FOREVER COOL

FOREVER COOL

HOW TO ACHIEVE

AGELESS, YOUTHFUL, AND

MODERN PERSONAL STYLE,

FOR WOMEN AND MEN

SHERRIE MATHIESON

CLARKSON POTTER/PUBLISHERS
NEW YORK

All rights reserved.
Published in the United States by Clarkson Potter/Publishers,
an imprint of the Crown Publishing Group,
a division of Random House, Inc., New York.
www.crownpublishing.com
www.clarksonpotter.com

Clarkson N. Potter is a trademark and Potter and colophon
are registered trademarks of Random House, Inc.

Originally self-published by Thompson Peak Publishing in 2006.

Library of Congress Cataloging-in-Publication Data is available
upon request.

ISBN 978-0-307-40531-9

Printed in China

Design by Arbor Books

10 9 8 7 6 5 4 3 2 1

First Clarkson N. Potter Edition

THANKS!

This book would not have been possible without its models, who gave of their
time so generously and left their egos at home, in support of my project.

It became a reality, thanks to the talent and creativity of Maria Makrynakis. Many thanks to Larry
Leichman, whose publishing "know-how" still guides me, and to Dennis Gorski for his editing skills.

Thanks to Kathryn Kay for her valuable help in organizing the chapters and facilitating
my thoughts to ring clear on the pages.

Also, to Ellen Barnes, for her cover photograph of me, a person
who's used to working *behind* the camera.

Personal thanks to my husband, John, for his unswerving belief in my talent. And,
of course, to my dear parents, on whom I can always count for truth and love.

CONTENTS

PART 1
Introduction

A UNIQUE VISION

We can run, but we can't hide from Mother Nature; sooner or later she catches up with us. But how do we deal with her when she does? You might have started thinking about aging when you were in your 30s; and most of us probably gave it serious thought during our 40s; but guaranteed, by the time we hit 50 it's a hot topic for all of us! With the media in our face shouting, "Don't age!" it's no wonder we're beating a path to the cosmetics counter to load up on empty promises or the plastic surgeon's door where we surrender to invasive procedures. Whether or not we go as far so a facelift, the bottom line is that we all want to *look* better.

I believe that looking better is about looking *natural*, and that aging gracefully is the only way to go. First and foremost, it's about embracing our age rather than denying it. Perhaps, for the first time since our teenage years, we can relax into being ourselves and accept the very things that make us unique. Then, it's about creating a personal style that expresses these qualities in a new way. Looking natural has nothing to do with that contrived look men and women "of a certain age" once aspired to (*stiff hair for both sexes, women with heavy make-up*). By combining a natural look with a modern perspective you can create a personal style that's unexpected, youthful and fresh.

My years as a costume designer, stylist, and style consultant have given me an extensive set of tools with which to identify a person's attitude toward fashion, find the roots of their aesthetic sense, and express their personality in a look that suits their lifestyle. While I have clients of all ages, I am particularly intrigued by the challenge that changing physiques and health issues pose for the over-50 crowd. The tools I offer in this book will help you reassess and reinvent your look while taking into account comfort, practicality, and style.

You'll see—*you can look your best through personal style alone!*

WHAT BECOMES "FOREVER COOL?"

What do I mean by cool? Certainly it doesn't mean wearing all and only black! Nor does it mean shouting to be seen or fading into the woodwork. Cool is knowing who you are and realizing your full potential. You'll know it when you see it—it's **ageless**, **modern**, and **youthful**.

Let me explain.

Ageless style is about transcending age by achieving a sense of *timelessness*—not being pegged by your age in any way. Ageless style mixes classic dressing with contemporary design to create a look that is refined and appropriate. It's never extreme, flamboyant, or funky, but it can definitely be imaginative and fun. It collects the best of the past and weaves in the new.

When you're **modern** it says that you're "of today"— that you know what's happening in fashion and trend. A modern look is the result of constantly reevaluating *your* look as you assess changing fashion to find what's appropriate for you. If you're modern, you're current.

When we think of **youthful** we think of words like active, energetic, vibrant, vital, dynamic…ideally, the way we feel. The aim of this book is *not* to make you look *young*. After all, you could learn how to dress like a trendy twenty-something by just flipping through magazines. My goal is to help you achieve a style that *implies* youthfulness. A youthful spirit is what we're after.

Keep in mind, too, that this is not a book on fashion; it's about style. Fashion is fleeting; style endures. Although style (the characteristic way we dress) is unique to each of us, it comes more easily to some than to others. This book will teach you how to *use fashion* to create an ageless, modern, and youthful style that works for you. In order to use fashion to your best advantage you need to understand the fundamentals. Just as it's important to master drawing if you're going to paint, it's essential to understand the concept of "classic dress" to create an ageless personal style. Build your look on a foundation of classic styles and it will serve you well through years of changing fashion trends. "Cool" has no expiration date!

OBSERVING COOL

Open your eyes! The next time you're out having a cup of coffee, before you bury your nose in the newspaper, take a page from the café societies of Europe and indulge in a little people watching. Be curious! Check out what they're wearing—do you like it, could you wear it? Don't miss it! Recognizing the style happening around you is essential to building a modern style of your own.

Whether you're in your 40s or have grandkids old enough to tell you what's cool, looking great is within easy reach. With the right tools you can create an ageless style that makes you look and feel amazing.

As you read, pay careful attention to the *before* and *after* photographs included. You will see that instead of models I've used real men and women with various body types—yours may be represented. The *before* photos feature outfits that we see every day; use them to discover the mistakes you might be making yourself. The *after* photos all demonstrate a modern solution; let them help you identify and create your best personal style. Each photo set reflects the chapter's theme and carefully explains its key points to help you understand the essentials of turning *never cool* into *forever cool*.

KEEPING OUR COOL

Let's face it, we all like looking good *and* we like the attention that comes with it. In fact, one of the hardest parts of getting older is feeling as if you aren't noticed as much as you once were… or as if you've fallen off the radar completely.

Over the years you've probably noticed fewer stolen glances and double takes aimed your way. If you spent your 20s and 30s watching slack-jawed waiters drop their trays, then it might be especially difficult to take. This is bound to be harder for some of us than others. Like it or not, the older we get the less our exterior matches our youthful inner spirit… until now.

Yes, we need to confront the realities of aging, but we don't need to feel defeated by it. Nor do we need to go to extremes. If you have always relied on your physical appearance for your sexual identity and have grown dependent on attention from the opposite sex, you may be tempted to choose inappropriate or provocative clothing in order to get yourself noticed. But, is that the answer? If we can put our self-worth, health, and fitness first, we can set a new benchmark for aging gracefully that is both positive and enduring.

THE MAN IN THE MIRROR

It often seems as if men have a better time of it. After all, they are able to procreate long after they've taken up shuffleboard, which undoubtedly gives their sexuality a boost. And what about those greying temples? While grey hair is almost never considered sexy on a woman, we often see these "silver foxes" attracting girls half their age. Even so, men do have their own struggles. Many find their receding hairlines and expanding waistlines distressing, and their vanity shouldn't be discounted. Regardless of gender, we can all benefit from a new perspective.

Looks *are* important—they affect how we feel about ourselves and how others relate to us. Luckily, we all have the potential to look great. A healthy lifestyle, a youthful attitude, and, yes, even good posture can take you far. Add great style to the mix and you'll have a new look that's as intriguing as anything you had in your younger years.

A STYLE IS BORN

HEIR APPARENT

If you spent any part of your adulthood in the '60s, '70s or '80s you've had to dodge quite a few fashion bullets. Our generation has had to contend with an overwhelming choice in what to wear, and the vast selection has led to much fashion confusion and many regrettable outfits. Fortunately, we have a style inheritance to fall back on. Take a look at a photo from the '20s, '30s, or '40s and you'll see that, when it came to negotiating fashion, it really was a simpler time. Both the wealthy and working class dressed in natural fabrics and followed the same rules of proper attire. Even people waiting in the breadlines looked presentable. The fact is, those generations benefited from a cohesive style that could never have allowed the indignities of, say, stirrup pants. We are the last link to an era of propriety and good taste, so let's draw on that heritage and pass it on down to our children. If not, we'll be squandering our style inheritance.

"IF YOU CAN'T BE A GOOD EXAMPLE...THEN YOU'LL HAVE TO BE A HORRIBLE WARNING!"

—Catherine Aird

FAMILY TIES

Although we as a generation have a collective heritage, as individuals we are more immediately influenced by our friends and family. Understanding the origins of your personal tastes is one of the first steps toward defining your style. How do you feel about fashion—totally apathetic, passionately obsessive, or somewhere in between? Just as we're born naked, we land in this world without a fashion sense, and from that moment on our education in aesthetics begins. Our most fundamental sense of aesthetics, that which stays with us long after we've left home, is determined by how our parents dressed, decorated, and socialized. As adolescents and young adults we may have rebelled against our parents' taste, but we eventually came back to the aesthetic values instilled by them.

THE COMPANY WE KEEP

Our families (fortunately) are not our only stylistic influences. Remember those rebellious teenage years, when you rejected your parents' tastes and adopted a style all your own? Chances are you relied on your friends and schoolmates to help you cultivate your new look. And, if you think about it, things haven't changed all that much since high school—we still turn to our peers for inspiration...and for confirmation. The people we know well (our friends and colleagues), as well as those we *think* we know from television and magazines, influence our choices in style. More often than not those people determine with whom we want to keep up, what we wish we had, and what's okay to wear. Our aspirations can refine us or not, depending on whom we choose to emulate—it's our choice.

THE GOOD, THE BAD, AND THE UGLY

Where, when, and with whom we live undoubtedly shapes our sense of style. But whether you feel those influences have put you ahead or held you back, your style is not set in stone. Think about who and what has shaped your taste; hold onto the best influences and let go of the rest.

Keep an eye out for new inspirations. When you go to the movies, pay attention to the wardrobe, notice the details that make it work. Buy high-end fashion magazines even if you can't afford what's in them—they'll help you develop an eye for style. As you flip through those pages decide for yourself which new trends are great (and might work for you)

and which will be on next month's *don't* lists. It's not just about clothes—reading books and magazines on art and architecture can give you a feel for proportion, color, texture, and design.

Most important, expand your horizons, and as you travel notice the styles (both good and bad) of the places you go. Instead of that snow globe, make a new style idea your souvenir! Our aesthetic education is an ongoing affair, and this time we get to choose our teachers. If you are committed to great style, you will never stop seeking out influence . . . or inspiration.

THE SUM OF ALL PARTS

I've always been a visual person, and there's nothing I like better than watching people—a pastime that manifested itself early on in my love of drawing and portraiture. Although I'd always had a keen interest in fashion, I never doubted that I would pursue a career in fine art until, in college, I discovered costume design. That discovery changed everything. In costume design I found the perfect union— a marriage between fashion and fine art. At 23 I passed my exam and was granted membership in the United Scenic Artists Union, which allowed me to work as a costume designer in film, theater and television. More important, it offered an opportunity to explore further the psychology of clothing—what we reveal to the world in what we wear.

As a costume designer I learned the art of creating character through wardrobe. To summon an identity with a past and a future, each detail of the costume had to have meaning—from collar to belt to those perfect shoes. These skills have served me well as a designer for film, television, music videos and commercials, and in styling for fashion magazines. Throughout my career I've had the good fortune to collaborate with talented directors like Ridley Scott and the opportunity to costume Academy Award winners such as Gregory Peck, Rod Steiger, Christine Lahti, and Susan Sarandon. I've also had the privilege of working with many other accomplished actors including Rita Wilson, Sela Ward, Jason Alexander, and Brooke Shields and

with sports legends Mickey Mantle, Joe Namath, and Sugar Ray Leonard, as well as music icons such as Billy Joel, Lena Horne, and the Judds.

Each of those great talents gave me an opportunity to create a persona through costume. Just as an actor dresses for a role in film, you can dress to express different aspects of your personality or a particular persona you might wish to project. It's a matter of deciding on what image you want to convey in your manner of dress and then carrying it off…with flair!

Today, I work in the private sector as a personal-style consultant with clients all over the country. I also travel and lecture on the many influences of style. My seminars include *The Psychology of Clothing, Cross-Generational Dress, Your Style Inheritance*, and *What Is Ageless Style*? The positive response to the seminars and the enthusiasm of my clients have emphatically demonstrated a need for this book.

AUNT RUTH—
A SOURCE
OF INSPIRATION

Although I didn't realize it at the time, the seeds for this book were sown many years ago when, at the age of sixteen, I visited my Aunt Ruth in Mexico City. She was German by birth, but had lived in many of the great cities of Europe and had a truly continental style. I stayed in her home, which was elegantly furnished with classic modern pieces. I was in heaven! Looking back I can say that Aunt Ruth was the first woman I really *looked at,* taking careful note of her style. It was understated and refined; she wore no makeup and she kept her stylishly short hair its natural color. My aunt dressed in classic styles and always wore flat, comfortable shoes. Her clothing was made of the highest-quality fabrics—always in a neutral palette—and her Mexican and Danish silver jewelry was of the latest modern design. Aunt Ruth made a profound and lasting impression on me—one that opened my eyes and taught me to recognize great taste.

It goes without saying that over the course of my life many things have influenced and inspired my sense of style. Some of those sources have led to enduring habits and tastes, some have been trends that only lasted a season, while others—a handful of individuals—have had a major part in shaping the way I think about style.

Millicent Rogers, a socialite who blazed new trails in fashion during the '30s and '40s truly mastered the art of the mix and made it her own. Her unique and often dramatic personal style always included an element of the unexpected. Mrs. Rogers was not shy about draping her tall, thin frame in voluminous ethnic ensembles, which she accessorized with great quantities of Native American jewelry—a look she pulled off with the utmost confidence.

If Mrs. Rogers adhered to the philosophy of "more is more," then Audrey Hepburn was definitely the mistress of "less is more." The lovely actress embodied elegance no matter what the occasion, never straying from her impeccable European Preppy look. Her contemporary, Cary Grant, was another to master simplicity in style. His understated look and his devotion to the well-tailored single-breasted suit should be inspiration for every man's wardrobe.

My commitment to the modern aesthetic is owed largely to Miuccia Prada. This awe-inspiring designer is the quintessential modernist, soaking up her own inspiration from every corner of the earth and from past fashion to create new designs that are eagerly anticipated and that set the trends for each new season. Her creative intelligence comes through in every piece in her imaginative use of fabric, color, and detail.

Ralph Lauren is one of the most enduring and accessible American designers. His appeal has a lot to do with his ability to play out, through style, a bit of the American Dream. From sportsmen to motorcyclists to movie stars and cowboys, Ralph Lauren is able to draw on the classics to which we are most attached and reinvigorate them with his own modern interpretation.

Years after my stay with Aunt Ruth I decided to draw a portrait of her from a favorite photograph. The drawing was intended as a gift and, at my mother's suggestion, I played down the lines on her face. When Aunt Ruth called to thank me, she said, "I love it! But you shouldn't have left out my hard-earned wrinkles!" Decades later her reply remained with me and, you might say, it was the first inspiration for this book, my philosophy on ageless style and what defines **Forever Cool!**

Forever Cool
Forever Cool
Forever Cool
Forever Cool
Forever Cool
Forever Cool
Forever Cool
Forever Cool
Forever Cool
Forever Cool
Forever Cool
Forever Cool
Forever Cool

THE ROAD TO FOREVER COOL

GET THE ROAD TO FOREVER COOL

THE ROAD TO FOREVER

FASHION HEALTHY COOL

THE ROAD TO

FOREVER COOL

THE ROAD TO THE ROAD TO FOREVER COOL GET
FOREVER COOL FASHION
HEALTHY

THE ROAD TO
FOREVER COOL

THE ROAD TO THE ROAD TO FOREVER COOL
THE ROAD TO FOREVER COOL

GET
FASHION

GET

FASHION
HEALTHY!

THE ROAD TO FOREVER COOL GET FASHION FASHION HEALTHY HEALTHY THE ROAD TO FOREVER COOL GET FASHION HEALTHY THE ROAD TO FOREVER COOL

18

It's no wonder people walk around dressed the way they do. Stores today are overflowing with badly made, gaudy styles that defy good taste (not unlike our supermarkets, packed as they are with unhealthy and overprocessed food). Due to this overwhelmingly vast selection, the task of choosing which bad clothes to use for the *before* photos became one of the more challenging aspects of putting this book together. As we age, it can be difficult to find appropriate, comfortable, practical and chic clothing amongst these toxic fashion trends. To that end, it is my intention to offer some remedies* I think you'll find easy to follow—and swallow.

   *Please follow this prescription as directed: When you look at the before and after photos in this book, make sure to read the tips carefully and completely—they contain vital nutrients for your "fashion health."

"Trickle-Down" Style

Don't worry if you can't afford haute couture (few of us can)—that's what "trickle-down" styles are for. This is a term for high fashion that has been copied or restyled by less expensive clothing and accessory lines. You can be sure that at the very moment a designer's latest idea comes down the runway, stylists are at the ready to reinterpret the design for public consumption—often resulting in a product that is remarkably well designed and made. The up side of trickle-down styles is its affordability. The challenge is that it can be difficult to find a unique look when there are so many similar styles on the market. In the comparison that follows you will see trickle-down style at its best; the result is a great look that doesn't break the bank!

(For brand names and resources, see Smart Shopping on p. 232.)

'COOL'
AT A
PREMIUM:

This brown corduroy, stretch cotton, safari-style jacket fits beautifully thanks to its sexy proportions. It combines nicely with slacks, as well as skirt looks. Versatility, great fabric, and a modern cut may justify its hefty $950 price tag (well...maybe).

'COOL' WITH 'TRICKLE-DOWN' STYLE

This very similar brown safari-style cotton jacket is a bit sportier and just as versatile. The fit is looser and less sexy, but otherwise has a very modern cut. Priced at $195, this jacket leaves you with money to spend on the rest of your outfit.

Cross-Generational Dress: The Art of the Mix

BORROWING THE LOOK

Do you feel like a younger you is trapped in an over-50s body? I know I do. While the days of miniskirts and skin-tight jeans may have passed you by, there are ways to express your youthful spirit without looking inappropriate. After all, it's probably not the miniskirt and tight jeans that you're really after, but the sense of personal expression and youthful sensuality that you so enjoyed. In this chapter you will learn how to recapture that aura of spontaneity, originality, and even a bit of sexiness by "borrowing" from the younger generation.

Of course it's important to consider carefully from whom you will be borrowing. Is there anyone in your family or social circle whose youthful look reflects a level of refinement and sophistication? If your daughter wears gobs of makeup and dresses in miniskirts, stilettos and haltertops, there's little mom or grandma can borrow…except what you shouldn't. Likewise, if your son won't leave the house without his underwear showing and his jeans dragging, Dad had better look elsewhere for inspiration.

Extreme examples aside, you will find there are many styles you can adopt from your son or daughter's wardrobe that will revive your youthful self-image while helping you to appropriately reinvent your look. Appropriate is the key objective here. Take stock of your physique; this means an honest appraisal in that full-length mirror.

UNDERSTANDING THE LOOK

The hallmarks of youthful style are its imaginative combinations and its unpredictability, which brings us to the art of the mix—the mix of modern and classic styles that have endured the test of time. An important principle to remember when revisiting past styles, as with current trends, is not to adopt the look as a whole, but to be selective. For example, it's okay to give nod to some of the fanciful fashions of the '60s and '70s by choosing an individual article of clothing or accessory and mixing it with something classic; that way you create a revision and not a rerun.

An exception to this is the Preppy look, which because of its classic roots and simplicity can be worn undiluted, as well as easily mixed. With its classic-cut jeans, button-down shirts, blazers, chinos, and polo shirts, it's a great example of an ageless style. Ralph Lauren, one of the most successful and enduring American designers, has built an empire on the Preppy principles, delighting his devotees, male and female, with a collection every year that reinvents and updates itself by adding a modern twist to the cut.

RETHINKING A WOMAN'S LOOK

One of the reasons that women's fashion trends repeat themselves is that they carry sexual undertones that can evoke a feeling of desirability. For example, "proportion-altering" styles used shoulder pads to widen the silhouette at the shoulders, creating the illusion of smaller hips; platform shoes added height and therefore lankiness; and let's not forget those animal prints forever associated with sensuality. Designers have over-indulged them all.

Fashion is a business with an agenda, and it's important to keep your own agenda in mind as you create your individual style. Designers turn out new collections for each and every season; weigh your choices carefully and shop wisely. Even if you can afford to buy the best of each year's designer collections, try to mix those pieces with less expensive items; you never want to appear to be trying too hard. You will find infinite opportunities for a sophisticated and modern look when you mix high-style pieces with simple ones. For example, the casual mix of a designer jacket with khaki chinos has an "arrived" look without being affected.

Now, what about those knit suits? At the very top, showcasing the best of this look, is the House of Chanel, which gave us the original ladylike suit in haute couture. But years of bad copies have made this prevalent style the territory of television anchorwomen and ladies who lunch. You know—those suits that no self-respecting daughter under 40 would be seen in or, for that matter, allow her mother to wear—unless she wants to wave a flag that says "matron." Adding to this uninspired look are the endless racks in U.S. department stores of "pre-mixed" ensemble outfits from established American firms. Being premixed, they deny you the option of creative combinations as they rarely go well with clothes from other designers. The best thing I can say for those clothing lines is that they often offer larger sizes (16 -18). Be careful: those premixed collections can make even the slimmest women look matronly. If you must choose an item or two from such collections, use a discerning eye to identify the pieces that allow for "the art of the mix."

If you keep your age and physique in mind you can have great success (and fun) borrowing from the younger generation's style. The only drawback is that the next time you're looking for that cute jacket, you might have to ask your daughter where it is!

The Art of the Mix

Never Cool

Under-age Looks:

Too sexy, glitzy, or cute is inappropriate for Mom.

Playing Dress Up:

Too much of a good thing will look like a costume.

Incorrect Accessories:

Never pair tailored accessories with ethnic clothing.

Forever Cool

Something Different:

Ethnic clothing can help keep things fun and interesting. The tunic top with its Moroccan roots is still a classic.

Creativity:

Express your creativity through imaginative color combinations and unique applique.

More Is More:

Jewelry can be stacked for a bolder look. More can be more when it's done well.

Finding Balance:

Pair ethnic tops with simple up-to-date pants or jeans.

Great Accessories:

Add individuality with great accessories in an ethnic style e.g., African, Native American, Asian, etc.

The Right Shoes:

Shoes must match the personality of the outfit (e.g., espadrilles, strappy sandals, thongs, etc.)

Never Cool

Improper Attire:

Avoid tops that are too revealing or tight—no bare bellies after 40!

Squeezing In:

No skin-tight jeans. Too sexual!

The Wrong Shoe:

High heels don't work with this casual look.

Overdoing It:

No heavy makeup or stiff hairdos with this fresh look.

Forever Cool

Creative Color:

Bold color gives punch to these classic polos.

A Perfect Fit:

These form-fitting shirts are sexy without being provocative.

The Right Bag:

This bright pink bag has a unique personality; it engages the eye and enhances the outfit.

Figure Flatterers:

The flare-leg, dark denim, and stretch of these jeans make them a figure-flattering choice for both mother and daughter.

The Right Shoe:

Moccasins and low-heeled sandals in a bright color can give a "fashion" look to a simple outfit.

Never Cool

Dated Cuts:

Never wear chinos with a high waist or a tapered leg.

Making Do:

Avoid poor-quality, stiff, or baggy shirts—especially tucked in.

Sad Accessories:

Get rid of boring or worn-out accessories.

The Wrong Shoe:

Don't wear high heels or pumps with this casual look.

Forever Cool

Reinvention:

Here classic Preppy gets some sex appeal.

Figure Flatterers:
Mom is covered but doesn't seem so.

Great Accessories:

Accessories are definitely cross-generational. Here's your chance to be expressive!

The Right Shoe:
Espadrilles and moccasins are a casual yet classy option.

Simplicity:
This form-fitting white shirt bridges the age gap and gives the outfit a classic foundation.

Combined Style:
A classic chino with a stylish twist always updates this look.

Something Special:
Good fabric, color, and fit make this simple outfit special. Layering this luxe green cashmere adds texture and a complimentary color.

Forever Cool

Never Cool

Overdoing it:

Avoid garish, glitzy, or showy jackets.

A Poor Fit:

Don't attempt this look with a baggy jacket or baggy pants.

Something Special:

This jacket makes the outfit. Its great color, pattern, and cut all make it special.

Figure Flatterers:

Mom is covered but her form is revealed.

Creative Color:

Green and orange are fun!

Combined Style:

Pair a feminine jacket with modern-cut jeans for a look that's soft but hip.

Great Accessories:

Accessories can't be over-emphasized—they can make or break your outfit!

RETHINKING A MAN'S LOOK

As you'll see in the photos that follow, borrowing from the younger generation is easily done. The trick is to learn to identify classic pieces and make them the foundation of your wardrobe. There are countless ways to update the look of basic jackets, shirts, slacks, and jeans by choosing modern cuts, interesting patterns, and great colors.

Certain designers and a select number of stores (see Smart Shopping section) are dedicated to offering men of all ages (limited only by their waistlines) the opportunity of adding excitement and a youthful spirit to their look.

Be sure to select wisely, avoiding the extreme trends that dominate today's youth culture. If you can balance your age and physique with the yearnings of a youthful spirit, you'll be well ahead of the game.

Never Cool

Dated Cuts:
Don't wear it over-sized if the current trend is fitted.

Mismatched Style:
Never pair this jacket with dressier slacks.

Forever Cool

Classics:
This jacket isn't too trendy and doesn't have an age limit. Pick a jacket in denim, corduroy, or simple, heavy-weight cotton—always in a current cut.

Combined Style:
For a classic mix, wear a jean jacket with a t-shirt, polo or western shirt. Pair it with jeans (as shown) or flat-front chinos.

The Right Shoe:
Keep footwear casual.

Never Cool

Squeezing in:

This goes for men too! Keep the look loose and easy.

The Wrong Shoe:

Men, like women, should avoid orthope-dic-looking shoes.

Forever Cool

Classics:

A great safari jacket has no age limit and it's both practical (those pockets) and masculine.

Simplicity:

This white shirt and navy t-shirt are simple and classic. A polo would be great, too.

Modern cuts:

Father and son are wearing flattering and hip, low-rise jeans.

The Right Shoes:

Shoes are sport/casual in a neutral tone.

Color That Works:

Khaki, white, and navy are masculine and easy to mix.

Forever Cool

Never Cool

Unfortunate Color:

Avoid yellow or ecru (cream) shirts—they do little for any complexion.

Color That Works:

Shirts in greens and blues look great on most men.

Finer Fabrics:

Do consider a well-cut shirt in a good cotton.

Never Cool

Overdoing it:

Don't wear over-styled shirts (ruffled, skin-tight, shiny fabrics) or with too many buttons undone.

Flashy Looks:

Don't wear tight designer jeans with obvious logos.

Forever Cool

Original Prints:

If your physique allows, choose a spirited shirt in an unexpected pattern (or color) but basic in cut.

Simplicity:

Pair it with well-cut jeans that aren't too trendy.

Acting Your Age:

Although your son might wear his shirt out, tuck yours in. Wear it without a belt for a more casual and effortless look.

The Right Shoe:

Shoes can be trendy, as with the "bowling" style shown (sneakers work, too).

Consistent Style:

Everything should look casual.

Introducing Our Models

Lura
AGE 75
PHILANTHROPIST
GRANDMOTHER

Lynn
AGE 50
ARTIST
MOTHER

Alexandra
AGE 55
ARTIST
MOTHER

Jennifer
AGE 20
STUDENT

Joann

AGE 64

SALES ASSOCIATE

GRANDMOTHER

Anita

AGE 50

MEDICAL SALES

MOTHER

Stephanie

AGE 61

FLIGHT ATTENDANT

GRANDMOTHER

Linda

AGE 55

REAL ESTATE AGENT

GRANDMOTHER

Bonnie

AGE 52

FINANCIAL

ADVISOR

Regina

AGE 52

NURSE

GRANDMOTHER

Nola

AGE 58

FLIGHT ATTENDANT

GRANDMOTHER

Helen

AGE 58

REAL ESTATE BROKER

GRANDMOTHER

Jean

AGE "FOREVER YOUNG"

PUBLICIST

GRANDMOTHER

Bob

AGE 56

HIGH SCHOOL

INSTRUCTOR

Adam

AGE 18

STUDENT

Mike

AGE 51

ARTIST/MANAGER

FATHER

George
AGE 56
HEALTH INSURANCE
EXECUTIVE
FATHER

John
AGE 53
TRUST AND ESTATE
SPECIALIST

Dan
AGE 52
FINANCIAL ADVISOR
FATHER

Jim
AGE 59
INSURANCE EXECUTIVE
GRANDFATHER

Rich
AGE 58
FINANCIAL ADVISOR
FATHER

Paul
AGE 57
CHIROPRACTOR
FATHER

Part 2

Women

SPORT–STYLE
"GOOD SPORTS!"

What were your parents doing at your age? Chances are they weren't doing three gym sessions a week or taking up white-water rafting. Our generation is definitely staying younger longer and, as a rule, we're pretty energetic. We already spend a significant amount of time being physically active (or think we should), and this is sure to increase as we head into retirement and a life of leisure. As a generation on the move, we love our casual, sporty clothes because they're comfortable and easy to wear.

Whether still working or retired, we all seem to pack a lot into our days. We often head out rather than home after the gym to run errands or meet a friend for breakfast. Think about how much time you spend in your exercise gear; those clothes are part of your wardrobe, not an exception to it.

You'll find that all the principles I've outlined so far are applied in the photos that follow. High-tech fabrics, great accessories, simple cuts, and terrific colors are all vital parts of your wardrobe. An active life provides many opportunities for a youthful sporty style, so grab the chance to create modern on-the-go looks. Sporty style, with the vitality it implies, could be your best style!

42

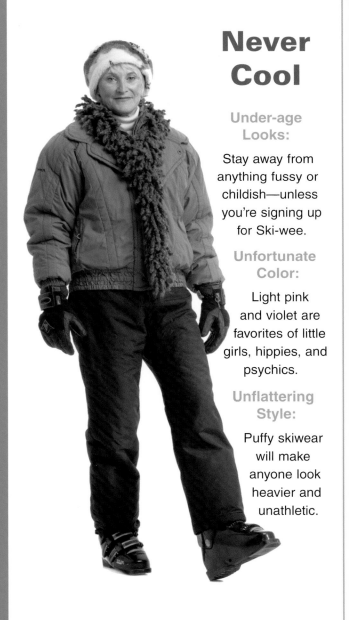

Never Cool

Under-age Looks:

Stay away from anything fussy or childish—unless you're signing up for Ski-wee.

Unfortunate Color:

Light pink and violet are favorites of little girls, hippies, and psychics.

Unflattering Style:

Puffy skiwear will make anyone look heavier and unathletic.

Forever Cool 1 & 2

Simplicity:

This simple, neutral palette lends sophistication to a sporty look.

Combined Style:

By starting with neutral basics you create the opportunity for endless combinations. For example, accessories or more colorful pieces can easily be added. You probably won't buy new outerwear every ski season, so leave yourself plenty of room for refreshing your look.

Finer Fabrics:

Buy quality pieces with good insulation (such as Thinsulate). You will stay warmer on the slopes and cut a slimmer figure than if you're piling on the layers under bargain ski wear.

Great Accessories:

Glasses and goggles offer another opportunity for sporty accessorizing.

43

Never Cool

Popping Out:

If your middle isn't your best feature, don't make it the main attraction.

Forever Cool

Figure Flatterers:

Choose a one-piece suit that covers strategically and streamlines the torso.

A Perfect Fit:

Wear a suit that has the shape and support you need.

Creative Color:

A black suit is usually a good choice, but consider how you might look in this gorgeous orange.

The Right Shoe:

Rubber thongs are lightweight and ideal for sand and water activities. As with any outfit, choose footwear that go with your suit.

THERE'S SURE TO BE A ONE-PIECE SUIT TO FIT AND STREAMLINE ANY FIGURE.

GOOD SPORTS

Never Cool

Hiding Out:

An oversized t-shirt might seem like a good option for the self-conscious, but it will only make you look oversized.

Unfortunate Color:

Please (except for Preppy style), don't buy pastels in anything larger than a 2T.

Overdoing It:

Stay away from clothing with glitter, sparkles, sequins, or cutesy sayings.

Making Do:

Treat yourself to a new pair of sneakers; they'll give you a fresh look and improve your workout.

Forever Cool 1

Simplicity:

Clean lines and a simple color scheme will create a sleek look.

The Right Bag:

Your gym bag is not an after-thought; it's an important part of the whole. It needs to hold all your gear, but you don't need to sacrifice style for function.

A Complete Look:

Choose a sporty jacket or hooded top to go over a trim exercise tee. You might not actually work out in this layer, but it will keep your appearance sharp when traveling to and from the gym.

Figure Flatterers:

Full-length exercise pants, like those shown, elongate the legs and give you the illusion of extra height.

The Right Shoe:

These fashion sneakers are great for taking you to a yoga or Pilates class in style. Choose a specialized athletic shoe for impact activities.

Forever Cool 2

Color That Works:

Color should definitely be kept simple; all black is always a safe bet.

Appropriate Attire:

This combo has slim lines without being too tight.

A Complete Look:

Both after photos illustrate looks that will serve you well before, during, and after your workout.

THE RIGHT "LONG" AND THE RIGHT "SHORT" OF IT—FALLS APPROPRIATELY AT MID-THIGH.

Never Cool

Making Do:

This tee must be left over from last decade's vacation.

Unfortunate Colors:

These colors are downright unsophisticated.

Unflattering Style:

Heavy cotton-knit ensembles (a staple of t-shirt shops) are stiff and bulky and not worth the cheap price.

Forever Cool

Simplicity:

Keep the look fresh, light, and clean.

Finer Fabrics:

A classic white t-shirt in quality cotton that won't loosen and sag will flatter your shape.

Appropriate Attire:

Wear shorts that are a decent length, taking into account your physique as well as what's appropriate.

Something Different:

These shorts, in a classic cargo style, provide a youthful look and are a welcome departure from ladylike pleated shorts.

The Right Bag:

A sporty designer bag carries the colors and maintains the simplicity of the look.

The Right Shoe:

Thongs are great for cooling feet and an ultracasual style.

Never Cool

Unflattering Style:

The ladies version of that tired Hawaiian motif (the same floral pattern men are so attached to).

Sad Accessories:

Bad colors, bad proportion—
bad taste!

Poor Fabrics:

Cheap synthetics never work.

AHH!
THE PURIST—
CLASSIC
AND
FRESH

Forever Cool

Flattering Style:
By keeping the pieces simple, well cut, and classic, she looks "classy."

Color That Works:
The hot-pink polo shirt adds punch to the clean, crisp, all-white look.

Finer Fabrics:
Always worth the extra cost; they look good and wear well.

The Right Shoe:
These golf shoes provide the latest technology and blend seamlessly with her outfit.

REALITY CHECK! REAL EXERCISE CALLS FOR PROPER GEAR.

Never Cool

Underage Looks:

These pants might as well say "Baby Doll" on the rear.

Unfortunate Colors:

This combination is harsh, and definitely not sporty.

Mismatched Style:

Since when do athletes wear lace?

Inappropriate Attire:

There's nothing wrong with looking attractive at the gym, but choosing a sexy look will only make you look inappropriate.

Unflattering Style:

These cotton knits hug her figure in all the wrong places, and it will only get worse when she breaks a sweat.

Forever Cool

A Complete Look:

Try a hip nylon jacket over your workout gear. A classic jean jacket or a zip-up sweatshirt (in a current cut) will also work.

Combined Style:

You don't need to buy a pre-matched set; choose colors and fabrics that work well for a pulled-together effect.

Great Accessories:

An attractively styled (plus appropriate) bag and shoes will add immeasurably to even the most casual outfit.

Simplicity:

Wear a hairstyle that is casual, low-maintenance, and flattering. Try a low or high ponytail (no pigtails!).

A Clean Look:

Wear little or no makeup. Obvious makeup doesn't fit the look and will start running as soon as you do.

Never Cool

Overdoing It:

Stay away from big and busy.

Unfortunate Color:

You may recognize this color scheme from your OB/GYN's waiting room. Remember, you don't need pink and purple to look feminine.

Sad Accessories:

Is she going to the gym or an audition for *Flash Dance*?

Unflattering Styles:

These three-quarter-length pants shorten the leg.

COVERED AND COMFORTABLE, HIP-SPORTINESS

Forever Cool

Better Fabrics:

Workout pieces in light-weight, high-tech materials will keep you comfortable at the gym. These hip, sport-specialized fabrics are less likely to ride up, bunch, or cling.

Simplicity:

A style that is simple and complements your physique is the goal.

Body Wise:

This zip-up top has a mock collar that provides an attractive frame and more coverage for an older neck.

Great Accessories:

Try a sporty watch with a nylon or rubber strap and clean, high-tech design. Your wedding band is the only other jewelry that should go to the gym.

Never Cool

Unflattering Style:

The cropped pants in this over-sized plaid exaggerate the hips.

Unfortunate Colors:

The combo of black, white, and pink is harsh with her coloring.

Bad Accessories:

Sun protection overkill!

The Wrong Shoe:

Those sensible brown golf sandals have definitely sacrificed form for function.

Forever Cool

Simplicity:

Clean lines and simple styling create a long, lean line.

Color That Works:

The blue palette is harmonious and fresh.

Great Accessories:

These blue-tinted sunglasses flatter her complexion and are the right proportion for her small face.

SIMPLE LINES ARE "PAR FOR THE COURSE!"

THE BEST COVER-UP STORY.

Never Cool

Under-age Looks:

A beach cover-up this cute belongs on a toddler.

Unfortunate Colors:

Avoid washed-out, drab colors—try hot, bright hues.

The Wrong Shoes:

The heavy black shoes look clumsy with this outfit.

Forever Cool 1

Figure Flatterers:

A sarong like this one will provide coverage without the bulk and is a classic poolside or beach cover-up.

Color That Works:

To maintain a long and lean silhouette, choose a print with coloring similar to your bathing suit.

The Right Bag:

An oversized straw bag like this one or a nylon tote is a fun option that will go with any suit and will hold all of your sun essentials.

Forever Cool 2

Figure Flatterers:

Long or short, a sarong will always be a classy cover-up solution. The length of your sarong should be determined by how much you wish to reveal.

Promising Prints:

This print works well for her (consider your figure, as prints can add weight).

CASUAL STYLE

"COMFORT ZONE"

Our lives today are more casual than ever. From catching a movie or lunch with friends, to shopping, dating, or traveling, our social calendars are filled with activities. But whether you're multi-tasking your way through life or enjoying leisure time, dressing casually is not a license for sloppiness or bad taste. Consider giving some thought to your casual wardrobe. If you follow a few guidelines you can achieve a style that's relaxed and seemingly effortless; there's no need to become a poster child for what not to wear.

From small country towns to big cities there are a number of things to take into consideration, especially weather and the physical challenges that it implies. Are you layering to keep warm or stripping down to be comfortable? It's possible to stay cool but still look appropriate and to bundle up without looking mummified.

The photographs that follow illustrate a vast selection of looks that offer opportunities for stylish dressing whatever your age, physical type, or personality. Wherever you live (or travel to) and whatever you're up to, these photos will help you select modern and sporty pieces that suggest action and imply youthful vitality. Comfort and great style are easily yours!

Never Cool

Unfortunate color:

Vegas here I come! This outfit is garish from head to toe.

Sad Accessories:

The Gold Rush is back on! This bag and shoe combo is the opposite of class.

Bad Accessories:

Red glasses are bad enough; that they match her outfit is even worse.

Forever Cool

Simplicity:

This style says "fresh and natural" instead of "old and tired."

The Right Fit:

Unconstructed, easy cuts (not oversized) are comfortable and not too demanding on the figure—a good choice for those of us who don't have perfect proportions.

Color That Works:

For an interesting look that isn't overwhelming, pair a top and pants in the same neutral tone (such as the white shown) and layer with a jacket in a contrasting color.

Figure Flatterers:

Here our eye is drawn to the shorter and darker denim jacket, a trick that makes this woman appear slimmer.

The Right Accessories:

This unique Native American necklace lends texture and fun to a simple outfit. Same goes for the bright straw and fabric bag.

The Right Shoe:

This flat shoe with a platform sole gives the woman height and makes her legs look longer.

Never Cool

Unflattering Style:

She looks convincingly pregnant in the voluminous top and pants.

Bad Accessories:

Those glasses! "All the better to see you with, my dear."

The Wrong Accessories:

Split personality—ethnic meets nursing home.

Forever Cool

Color That Works:

Choose tones that work with your coloring. Here her gorgeous silver hair is beautifully accented.

Figure Flatterers:

These simply styled pieces don't cling or bunch. Fabrics that skim the body will ensure a slimming silhouette.

The Right Accessories:

The turquoise, alabaster, and silver cuff bracelet is a beautiful detail that adds a bit of color and a hint of personal creativity.

The Right Shoe:

This style fits perfectly with the overall simplicity of the look.

Never Cool

Unfortunate Color:

Colors for a senior moment—even her watchband is pink!

Bad Hair Day:

This all-too-popular short and permed hairstyle may be inexpensive and practical, but it is never attractive.

NATURAL FIBERS AND UNEXPECTED COLOR COMBINE FOR CREATIVE STYLE.

Forever Cool

Creative Color:

The combination of bright orange and gold (think sunset) gives this wearer a warm glow. Even bright colors can be combined for a sophisticated monotonal effect.

Simple Beauty:

This simple hairstyle allows a lovely face to shine!

Figure Flatterers:

The pieces in this outfit have an easy drape. They create a body-skimming effect, but are just loose enough to get all the necessary coverage.

Great Accessories:

Stacked wood and jewel bracelets add interesting detail, texture, and a bit of personality. The straw and fabric tote brings out the colors of the outfit and adds a few of its own.

The Right Shoe:

Beige flats would also be fine, but these in orange are less expected and a bit more fun.

Never Cool

Squeezing In:

You'll attract men, but not the ones you want.

Unflattering Style:

The clinginess of this outfit only adds weight.

Sloppiness:

Looking as if you've just rolled out of bed is only appropriate for that short time between morning alarm and morning shower.

WHOA! BUSTIN' OUT ALL OVER!

"BUTTONED-UP": MODERN AND **SEXY** ON ALL COUNTS.

Forever Cool

Color That Works:

An all-black outfit is always hip; try it with dark stretch jeans like these.

Figure Flatterers:

This long, slim shirt hugs her body without revealing too much.

The Right Shoe:

Flat bowling-style shoes are comfortable and stylish—a perfect fit with this all-black ensemble.

The Right Bag:

A nylon bag has a basic and versatile style that's perfect for a casual outfit. As an added bonus, it's also lightweight and comfortable to carry.

Never Cool

Overdoing it:

She's been upholstered!

Unflattering Style:

These jeans wouldn't flatter any legs.

Sad Accessories:

Did she get that plastic tote free with her cosmetics?

More Sad Accessories:

Those owlish frames have got to go.

The Wrong Shoe:

They may be comfortable—but they're painfully sensible.

CASUAL STYLE
CASUAL STYLE
CASUAL STYLE
CASUAL STYLE
CASUAL STYLE
CASUAL STYLE
CASUAL STYLE
CASUAL STYLE
CASUAL STYLE
CASUAL STYLE
CASUAL STYLE
CASUAL STYLE
CASUAL STYLE

Forever Cool

Something Special:

If you can pull off the look, a cool hat will always be a great choice.

Simplicity:

This buttery leather coat's easy style makes the outfit.

Figure Flatterers:

Choose jeans in slimming dark denim; they have a slight stretch for a better fit.

Great Accessories:

These accessories have a country feel and work well within the color palette; they "go" in all respects.

Never Cool

Overdoing It:

These prints should definitely be caged.

Squeezing In:

With clothing this tight, the men will certainly be looking; they might be trying to figure out if you're a "working girl."

Sad Accessories:

Mr. T called; he'd like his jewelry back.

The Wrong Bag:

Bronze, pewter, or gold bags should rarely be resurrected.

An Unnatural Appearance:

Teased hair and heavy makeup go perfectly with this look.

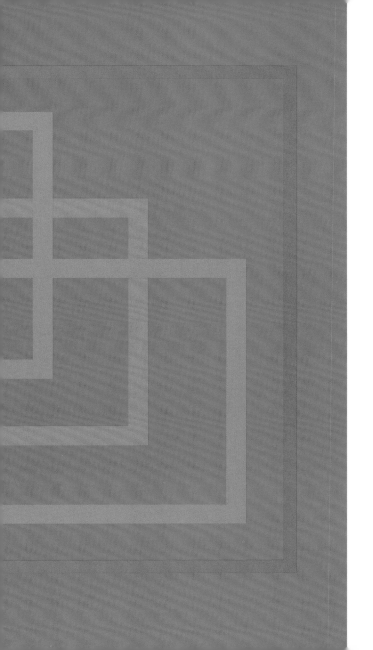

Forever Cool

Simplicity:

A classic example of "less is more."

Natural Beauty:

A current hairstyle and minimal makeup lets her loveliness through.

Figure Flatterers:

These black slacks in a fine wool have no pleats and a slightly wide leg for a slimming cut.

Never Cool

Nonsense Style:

The pieces in this outfit just don't work together. Maybe she has multiple personalities.

Sad Accessories:

This ladylike hat is downright silly.

Unflattering Styles:

That top she picked up in the Juniors Department can do nothing to save her dated and poorly cut jeans. This outfit adds pounds, but not style.

The Wrong Shoe:

Her black platforms stand out like a sore thumb (as does the black bag).

DO NOT BECOME A "MAD HATTER"!

Forever Cool

A Complete Look:

She is wearing a look that says "western" without looking like a costume—it's youthful, yet appropriate.

Great Accessories:

A few unusual accents can transform a plain white tee and jean combo into a stylish look with real personality.

Something Special:

This trendy yet classic cowboy hat will keep her "cool" in more ways than one.

The Right Shoes:

The shoes offer an understated and comfortable alternative to a predictable boot, and the platform adds height.

Figure Flatterers:

These low-slung and slightly flared dark denim jeans have a slimming effect. Take another look at that before photo and you'll really appreciate them!

Never Cool

Squeezing In:

This skin-tight top reveals too much information!
She may as well be wearing a leotard.

Underage Looks:

Cutesy denim skirts should never have gotten past the eighth grade. Long or short, they're not for you.

Inappropriate Attire:

Even if you have great legs, a skirt this short is off limits.

Forever Cool

Combined Style:

A tunic top and easy pant combo is a classic look for summertime.

Creative Color:

Coral is punchy and fun, and almost universally flattering.

Great Accessories:

Summer is a great season to bring out those funky, ethnic or colorful accents. Collect these accessories as you come across them; they'll always come in handy for spicing up simple warm-weather styles.

Figure Flatterers:

This long tunic will look good on any physique and can moonlight as a beach cover-up.

EVEN IF YOU STILL HAVE GREAT LEGS... ABOVE-THE-KNEE SKIRTS ARE A "NO, NO!"

Never Cool

Dated Looks:

The wide-shouldered leather coat is strictly '80s vintage. Try selling it on eBay.

Unflattering Style:

What once was considered sexy today looks harsh and severe.

The Wrong Shoe:

Oh, whom are we kidding? With a coat this ugly, no one will even notice.

Forever Cool 1

Creative Color:

Monochromatic doesn't have to be boring! This outfit plays with different shades of the same color for an interesting effect.

Appropriate Attire:

This lightweight, stylish jacket doesn't skimp on the warmth or comfort. It can take you from the city to the ski lodge.

The Right Shoe:

These short leather boots are flat and comfortable; they're truly "made for walking."

Forever Cool 2

A Classic Revisited:

This wool jacket is a sophisticated and stylish update of the standard trench coat.

Color That Works:

An all-black combination of a ribbed wool turtleneck and velvet jean-cut pants creates long and lean effect.

The Right Shoe:

A simple black leather boot (with a manageable 1-1/2" heel) is a sleek style for a sporty urban look.

Forever Cool 3

Something Special:

This leather jacket is a high-fashion interpretation of an American classic: the motorcycle jacket. You'll have to have the right physique and attitude, but if you can pull it off, it's a great look.

Finer Fabrics:

The soft, beautiful leather gives this piece sophistication.

Combined Style:

Notice that the rest of her outfit is sporty and low key. If you've got a jacket this special, let it take center stage.

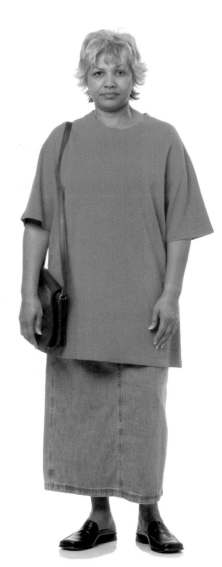

Never Cool

Hiding Out:

Wearing clothing this oversized will make you look like a linebacker in a skirt!

Unflattering Style:

This long denim skirt is never the right choice, not even at a square dance.

Unfortunate Color:

Unless you're a bullfighter, steer clear of reds this bright.

Forever Cool

Simple Style:

The fresh look of a colorful blouse is relaxed and will suit anyone.

Figure Flatterers:

These white slacks are cut like jeans with a slight flare. They slim her hips and elongate her legs.

Great Accessories:

Choose accents that will enhance your outfit's color scheme.

Never Cool

Overdoing it:

She has crossed the line from western influence to cowgirl costume.

Faking it:

This fake Concho belt and pink boots couldn't look less authentic.

GIVING "WESTERN" A BAD NAME.

Forever Cool

A Classic:

Western shirts are a hip choice and come in many different fabrics and colors.

Something Fun:

Western done well is refreshing and relaxed.

A Good Fit:

These chinos (in a current cut) combined with a fitted shirt create a slim line.

Great Accessories:

An authentic Concho belt or a great pair of vintage cowboy boots would be a great investment.

Never Cool

Unflattering Style:

A little more fabric and this shapeless dress could be a muu-muu.

Bad Accessories:

If it's a shawl, wear it like a shawl (around both shoulders). The bone bag and "comfy" matching loafers have added 20 years to her look.

Over-age Looks:

The pink glasses on the tip of her nose just added another 10 years.

THE ARTSY SENIOR "TOGA" LOOK.

SOFT, NATURAL AND ARTISTIC STYLE.

Forever Cool

Color That Works:

The cooling white and soft cream flatter her natural coloring and create a refreshing look.

The Right Accessories:

This silver "squash-blossom" necklace blends with the outfit and evokes an artistic personality.

Finer Fabrics:

The beautiful textures of the linen pieces and varied fabric weights enhance and provide visual interest.

The Right Shoe:

These driving moccasins work especially well with a soft, casual, and comfortable outfit.

Never Cool

Unflattering Style:

If a cardboard box were made of leather, it would look like this jacket.

Unfortunate Color:

I don't think she even thought about color.

The Wrong Cut:

These jeans are more like denim pants. Their ladylike cut adds weight and subtracts style.

The Wrong Shoe:

These fake moccasins in a cutesy, wedged style must be from Teepee Town.

The Wrong Bag:

This is an old-lady bag, perfect for getting help crossing the road or beating a would-be mugger.

CHIC

LAYERING

OF TEXTURE

AND

COLOR.

Forever Cool

Simplicity:
This olive boucle-wool coat is a classic cut with an easy and unconstructed shape.

Color that Works:
The light green turtleneck and the multicolor print cashmere shawl complement one another and brighten the outfit.

Combined Style:
Layering a soft wool shawl over your coat can add dimension and color.

Great Accessories:
The shoes and bag are of fine, soft leather. Their sleek design complements a look that is clean and modern.

COLOR CAN "MAKE" OR "BREAK" YOUR LOOK.

Never Cool

Unflattering Style:

This matching outfit makes her look as if she's off to work in a nursing home.

Unfortunate Color:

Buyer beware! Teal is a risky '80s investment.

Forever Cool 1

Something Fun:

If you have the arms for it, this top (by a design house famous for its colorful prints) can be an appropriate and stylish option.

Figure Flatterers:

These dark denim stretch jeans that ride low (not too low) lengthen the torso for a slimming effect.

The Right Shoe:

Espadrilles (wedged or flat) are a light and lovely summer option.

Forever Cool 2

Color That Works:

Bold, bright blocks of color give this light-weight top a playful and fashionable spirit. A simple long-sleeved design, like this one, is great for a small frame.

Combining With Style:

These white ankle-length pants are a refreshing complement to the bright shirt.

Great Accessories:

This man's silver watch adds no-nonsense sportiness and the simple black accents highlight the top.

Never Cool

Hiding Out:

This giant sweater is still managing to cling, with an enlarging (and alarming) effect on the wearer.

Unflattering Style:

We can tell these stiff chinos are poor quality. They definitely don't fit and they seem to be piling up around her ankles.

Unfortunate Colors:

When did the bone (or white) bag and shoe combo become a "must have" for spring and summer?

The Wrong Shoe:

These lace-ups say "orthopedic."

Forever Cool

Something Special:

This classic serape, in an understated color, is as comfortable as a jacket or shawl and creates a dramatic, stylish effect.

Combined Style:

A simple brown turtleneck and slim-legged suede pants provide warm color and great texture. They are a perfect complement to the bold serape.

Great Accessories:

Silver earrings fit well with the ethnic style of this look.

The Right Shoe:

The comfortable beige suede moccasins work with the outfit's palette and add a bit of western character.

THE DIFFERENCE BETWEEN

"BLAND AND BORING"

AND

CLASSIC

SIMPLICITY.

Never Cool

Unflattering Style:

Here comes Plain Jane.

Dating Yourself:

An outfit this dated belongs in the thrift shop.

Boring Attire:

Her conservative streak has taken over!

Forever Cool

A Classic:

This safari look manages to be both practical and feminine.A hip and ageless style.

Color That Works:

You can keep the palette neutral and add black for an edgier look.

Practical Considerations:

This outfit is the answer to a traveler's prayers.

Never Cool

Unflattering Looks:

This mostly black, harsh, heavy-duty look is usually seen on a motorcycle.

Bad Combinations:

The jeweled denim jacket is as garish as the t-shirt—bad pieces even worse when combined.

Wrong Accessories:

Bags with designer initials had better be the real thing! Buy them for style and quality, not snob appeal.

Bad Hair:

This hair could use a wash and conditioning.

Forever Cool

Something Special:

Cashmere and a bit of mink detail on the hood lend luxe, while the sporty cut keeps the style casual.

The Right Bag:

This newsboy bag in wool felt adds a youthful spirit.

Color That Works:

Keeping the palette neutral and toned down is the key to a sophisticated and understated look.

The Right Shoe:

These black flat half-boots provide the look and comfort required.

A CHOICE:

HARD-EDGED

AND "LOW-DOWN"

OR SLEEKLY

FEMININE

AND UNDERSTATED.

Never Cool

Unflattering Style:

Broad stripes and a baggy cut don't cut it!

Sad Accessories:

And we thought gold chains were bad on men!

A Bad Cut:

This pair of jeans comes with an extra 20 pounds in the pockets.

The Wrong Bag:

This conservative black purse (not to mention those sensible sandals) sticks out like a sore thumb.

Making Do:

Last, but definitely not least, what's with the upswept hair?

Forever Cool

Simplicity:

Combining neutral colors can have a lovely effect. These pieces are also easy to mix for other casual combinations.

A Youthful Look:

This jacket and pants combo is a prime example of cross-generational dressing.

Figure Flatterers:

Low-slung jeans provide the illusion of slimmer hips.

Natural Beauty:

If you've got hair this beautiful and shiny, keep it long and wear it down.

Never Cool

Unfortunate Color:

Save pink for the PG crowd (unless you're doing Preppy).

Sad Accessories:

The white bag and pink shoes look like icing on a cake.

"5 EASY PIECES"= TOTALLY UNCONTRIVED.

Forever Cool

Color That Works:

It's amazing what the right shade can do for a gal! Green is extremely versatile. It works well with both warm and cool tones.

Simplicity:

This short cotton number is as classic as any denim jacket and combines well with casual slacks or jeans.

Great Accessories:

Summery accessories don't have to be bright. These neutral tan accents provide a light feel.

"WHAT WORKS!"

Whether you are looking for a job, a promotion, or reinventing yourself in a new career, the fact remains that the workplace is increasingly competitive. First impressions are important, and in the case of getting and keeping a job they are crucial. In order to show that you are up to the task, you've got to look the part. In today's society if you look old, people are going to assume that you think old. When you see someone dressed in a modern, hip fashion you presume that they're up on today's world—it's as compelling as it is attractive.

Of all places, the workplace is the environment in which you will want to make sure that you are dressing appropriately. Regardless of your profession or how casual the dress code, being unfamiliar with or naïve about what's appropriate is just plain unsophisticated.

Although we're bombarded with sexy images in magazines and on film, showing too much skin in the workplace can lead to not being taken seriously; at the very least, you will come off as insecure. You don't want to be the topic of conversation around the copy machine.

Commanding respect is especially key to executive style and those who aspire to it—but that doesn't require a wardrobe of boring suits. Try for something less predictable, as illustrated in the photographs that follow. Regardless of which look you choose, give careful thought to color and a good cut, and remember that quality fabrics can do a lot for aging skin. Dressing stylishly carries an aura of creativity and self-confidence; you'll see, it makes all the difference!

Never Cool

Improper Attire:

No short skirts or revealing necklines in the office.

Inappropriate Ornaments:

Overly ornate earrings, ankle bracelets, childlike barrettes, or other silly accessories.

Bad Hair:

Avoid hairstyles that are too young or sexed-up (overly teased or bleached hair).

Forever Cool

A Perfect Fit:

Wear a simple dress that flatters your figure; the one shown is a classic shirtdress in an unexpected print.

Helpful Hemlines:

The best skirt length hits you at the knee or a bit below.

Great Accessories:

Choose shoes and belts (if needed) that enhance the overall look and are stylistically correct.

Colors That Work:

Neutrals are sophisticated and easy, but a great color can add that "wow" factor.

Never Cool

Dated Suits:

Two words: Salvation Army.

Unfortunate Colors:

This '80s teal does nothing to enhance her look.

Problem Prints:

This windowpane check is too masculine and boring.

The Wrong Bag:

Don't spoil your outfit with Grandma's handbag.

Dainty Jewelry:

Pearls (real or fake) can work if they are classic, exotic, or make a statement (good size and luster).

Comfort Shoes:

Avoid shoes that are nothing but sensible. There are plenty of choices out there and you needn't sacrifice style for comfort.

Dated Eyewear:

Make an effort to choose glasses that add style, not years.

STAY COMPETITIVE! THINK MODERN.

Forever Cool

Coordinated Pieces:

Wear casual suits that let you mix and match in neutrals as shown.

Finer Fabrics:

Choose classic/modern shapes in quality fabrics. Here, wool crepe provides a beautiful, languid ease.

An Eye for Detail:

Pick a jacket with three or more buttons for a youthful look; one button will make you look matronly.

The Right Shoe:

Wear a boot in cooler weather—it looks streamlined and modern. (Good camouflage for heavier legs.)

Great Accessories:

Try a masculine watch—here, over-sized in silver.

The Right Bag:

Buy a neutral-colored bag that is large enough for your needs but still attractive—a leather/canvas combination makes it multi-seasonal.

Modern Eyewear:

Opt for glasses in an up-to-date style.

Simplicity:

Keep your look simple and seemingly effortless.

COMFORT AND STYLE ARE NOT MUTUALLY EXCLUSIVE.

Never Cool

Up-tight Pieces:

Any blouse closed at the neck; it's almost as bad as a bow at the collar.

Unfortunate Colors:

Pastels (only great for a Preppy look) are super for babies but too often embraced by seniors.

Comfort Shoes:

Sneakers are never a good solution with any skirt suit—there are many stylish options when comfort is the issue.

Forever Cool 1

Coordinated Pieces:

The black leather blouse/jacket is classic and fun— great for mixing.

The Right Shoe:

When choosing a skirt, think about the shoes; they can be comfortable (flat or low heel) but must work stylishly with the outfit.

Great Accessories:

The vintage Mexican bracelet adds interest and character without flash.

Forever Cool 2

Creative Colors:

The color of this short, well-cut leather jacket has a trendy "ombre" effect and will remain modern for a long while. The citrus-yellow tank gives punch.

Appropriate Attire:

For a professional look— chic, fluid, black slacks are a neutral compliment to this leather jacket that makes a statement.

The Right Bag:

The quilted black bag lends a needed soft-ness to the look.

The Right Combination:

Slacks, in general, allow for more shoe options (including flats for comfort).

MINIMALIST AND MONO-TONE= A "TOTAL LOOK" THAT IS VISUALLY ENGAGING.

Never Cool

Predictable Pieces:

Too conservative and boring.

Underage Looks:

This is an outdated "school days" hairstyle.

Unfortunate Color:

Bland colors do nothing for the outfit or the woman.

Forever Cool

Colors That Work:

You can wear all white in summer as often as you wear all black year-round.

A Perfect Fit:

If you are petite, the monotone elongates and flatters the figure.

Simplicity:

The minimalist look is modern, uncomplicated, and perfect on her small frame.

Good Grooming:

Healthy, shiny hair is terrific—why not wear it loose and longer? Show it off!

Never Cool

Dated Suits:

With only one button it becomes matronly (poor-quality fabric doesn't help).

Unfortunate Colors:

Watch out for colors that fade you.

Predictable Pieces:

This little silk top with a jewel neckline inspires nothing but yawns.

The Same Old Bag:

Carrying the same bag every day doesn't accommodate changing outfits and conveys a lack of style.

Comfort Shoes:

Avoid anything orthope-dic-looking and keep in mind that white or cream shoes will age you—try black, brown, or tan (even in summer) with a bag of similar color.

"SAME OLD, SAME OLD!"

FUN, HIP, AND FEMININE.

Forever Cool

Coordinated Pieces:
Wear a wool/silk twin set with a current, fitted cut.

Color That Works:
A bright, punchy color like this coral will add life to your complexion.

Youthful Alternatives:
The sweater set is a viable, modern alternative to a jacket, and a good Casual Friday option.

Creative Combinations:
The fun graphic of this skirt works well and adds an edge to the classic twin set.

A Perfect Fit:
The skirt's style and length are just right for this woman.

The Right Shoe:
The sleek and simple pump with 1-1/2" heel is classic, modern, and comfortable.

BRIGHT "PREPPY"

COLORS CAN

SEPARATE YOU

FROM THE CROWD.

Never Cool

Predictable Pieces:

Don't hide in an oversized, conservative raincoat.

The Wrong Bag:

Plain Jane accessories say, "Please ignore me."

Forever Cool

Creative Colors:

Push to be adventurous! Even if you are conservative, color can be your inspiration.

Great Accessories:

The white blouse and tan sandals tone down the colorful outfit.

Never Cool

Dated Suits:

Again, a matronly mix-and-match suit with gold buttons. Poor cut, poor color, and poor pattern. Next!

Dainty Jewelry:

This one-strand, dainty necklace adds nothing to the look.

The Wrong Bag:

Yikes! There's that bag again.

Short Slacks:

These slacks fall short by exposing the entire shoe.

SIMPLICITY AND QUALITY ADD UP TO A REFINED LOOK.

Forever Cool

Simplicity:
This fitted black turtle-neck with olive wool slacks presents a slimming silhouette.

The Right Bag:
An investment-quality bag promises to be modern and useful for many years—shown here in a rich, dark-brown leather.

Great Shoes:
These boots com-plement the color scheme and relate to the bag.

Appropriate Attire:
Great option for Casual Friday or a less formal office job.

Never Cool

Unfortunate Colors:

Jewel tones (think burgundy, gold, emerald) are aging colors. This burgundy suit is obvious proof.

A Poor Fit:

A double-breasted jacket is never as flattering as one that is single-breasted (and looks sloppy if worn open).

Predictable Pieces:

This under-blouse is uninspired and severe, contributing to an outfit that is hard-edged and aging.

The Wrong Shoes:

With rare exception, avoid matching your shoe color exactly to your outfit (unless it's black).

A "MUST-HAVE" PANTSUIT FOR ALL SEASONS.

Forever Cool

Simplicity:

This classic, well-cut suit is "black magic" at its best. Black makes life simple and is easy to mix. (It's a forgiving color that lets lesser-quality fabrics pass inspection.)

A Perfect Fit:

This has a youthful "hunting jacket" effect because it's form-fitting with multiple buttons.

Creative Colors:

The green turtleneck gives punch to the outfit.

The Right Bag:

The soft green leather bag works with the turtleneck and adds an element of surprise.

The Right Shoes:

Shoes and boots that blend in add length to the leg, as do pointy shoes.

Never Cool

Matronly Suits:

This ladylike knit is sure to age you (and no gold buttons, please!)

Primary Colors:

They belong in kindergarten. Don't wear them—especially with black slacks or skirts.

Dainty Jewelry:

The gold clip-on earrings, pin, and necklaces do little more than add glitter; file them with the gold buttons.

Short Slacks:

It's difficult to look profession-al in slacks that come up short. Exposing tan stockings only makes it worse.

The Wrong Bag:

This ladylike structured bag only adds more stiffness.

Scary Hair:

This includes all varieties of over-spraying, "helmet hair," and "big hair."

LADY-LIKE KNITS ENSURE AN OLDER LOOK.

Forever Cool

Simplicity:
Edit your look with a current fit and flattering style.

Color That Works:
Neutral colors are always sophisticated and mix easily.

Finer Fabrics:
Buy the best. Their flattering effect (as we age) is worth the money.

Coordinated Pieces:
Wear a two-piece outfit that appears suited rather than matching; it suggests a more relaxed feel.

Great Accessories:
Think quality and style; great accessories can make the outfit, especially shoes and bags.

A Perfect Fit:
Make sure that every part of your outfit fits well. If something's not quite right, don't buy it—or make sure it's properly altered.

Like New:
Keeping your clothing and accessories in tip-top condition is essential.

Never Cool

Dated Suit:

You can't resurrect it!

Unfortunate Colors:

There is no color cohesion here.

The Wrong Bag:

This bag is way too large and cumbersome.

THINK FRESH! THINK WHITE WITH COLOR COMBOS!

Forever Cool

Creative Colors:

This shorter, three-button jacket is a sophisticated shade of green.

Simplicity:

These slacks fit well and the fresh white gives the outfit sparkle.

Great Accessories:

The tan bag carries the stripe of the jacket and provides a spring/summer look.

Never Cool

Unfortunate Colors:

Just a bad color combination

Dated Suits:

They abound, and love to hang around.

Forever Cool

A Perfect Fit:

A long, lean, monotonal outfit is slimming; you'll never tire of it.

Appropriate Attire:

This two-piece outfit works for Casual Fridays.

Coordinated Pieces:

This shirt-jacket and slacks combo can be easily mixed and imaginatively accessorized to change the look of the outfit.

Great Accessories:

The accessories and the color of this outfit are harmonious.

"ISN'T SHE LOVELY?"

Most women enjoy dressing up. A big part of why we look forward to lunch with the girls, dinner at a posh restaurant, or an evening at the theatre is because of the clothes we get to wear. It's an opportunity to express our individuality with a bit of sensuality. Yes, dressing a bit sexier for those events is apropos. But what's appropriate? No matter how tempting it is to please your spouse or date, who thinks you have the best legs or the loveliest décolletage on earth, trust your own good sense when it comes to where your dress should begin and end. Even if you've managed to maintain the weight you were in high school, the rules have changed. It's time to be subtler and more refined.

But, what works for you now?

The answer lies in honest self-appraisal. Learning to highlight your best features (every woman has her share) and disguise your less attractive attributes is an important skill to master at any age. As you'll see in the photographs that follow, there are exciting options for every physique. From sleek and minimalist to eccentric or ethereal—it's your chance to be a knockout!

Never Cool

Prissy Looks:

This sweater is just too cutesy; it looks like a doily.

Unflattering Style:

These long floral skirts are no better than the dress version. They are the ultraconservative interpretation of femininity.

The Wrong Shoe and Bag:

The unfortunate styles of this shoe and bag can be bought in every mall, but why buy them?

Forever Cool

Combined Style:

This is a classic sweater set (popular since the soda-shop days of the 1950s) with a modern twist. A set like this one is a great alternative to a jacket, sweater, or shawl when you need a bit of coverage.

Color That Works:

This coral-red is like a booster shot for the complexion.

Flattering Style:

The multiple strands of coral create a lovely neckline and make a real statement, supporting the color scheme and adding texture.

A Classic:

Camel lightweight wool slacks are a wardrobe staple, especially in this classic proportion.

Great Accessories:

These understated accessories, also in camel, don't overpower the "good thing" she's got going.

Never Cool

Under-age Looks:

Senior Prom, at best.

Unnatural Beauty:

Blue eye shadow and pale, frosted lipstick make a not-so-sweet sixteen.

REALITY CHECK!

UNDERSTATED AND SEXY, WITH A 'WOW' FACTOR.

Forever Cool

Color That Works:

This white ensemble with a bit of black has a 'wow' factor as powerful as any bright colors could produce!

Versatile Style:

This outfit, great for an afternoon party or wedding, is composed of versatile pieces (see "Black-Tie," p.147, for a transformation).

Natural Beauty:

If you've got amazing hair, flaunt it by wearing it long and loose.

Never Cool

Unfortunate Style:

She needs a cure for the "common old." Outfits like these are epidemic.

Sad Accessories:

Could the glasses get any bigger?

GET OVER "THE COMMON OLD"!

Forever Cool

Something Special:

This hand-painted Kimono-style top is unique and understated.

Figure Flatterers:

This design has an elegant drape, a good choice for a physique that suffers in more structured pieces.

Practical Style:

Ease, comfort, and beauty to spare.

Combining With Style:

The fluid black slacks create a graceful line and won't compete with her beautiful top.

Great Accessories:

A gorgeous Asian-inspired necklace relates well to her ensemble and lends some excitement to her neckline.

Never Cool

Inappropriate Attire:

This look sends a message loud and clear! Men will respond predictably.

Under-Dressed Style:

This outfit is a great way to catch a chest cold.

The Wrong Shoe:

These boots are made for walkin' . . . the streets.

Overdoing It:

Punky, teased hair and obvious makeup just make it worse.

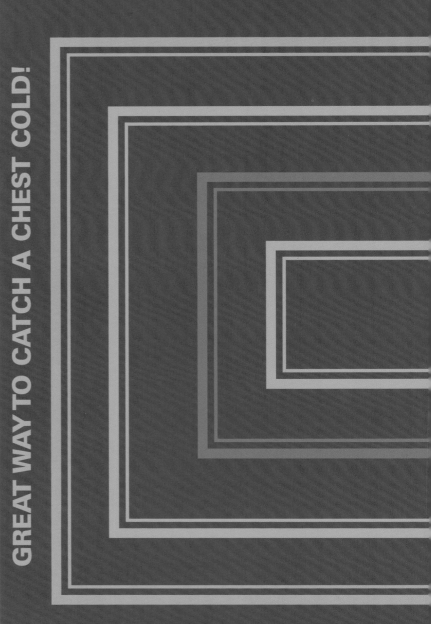

GREAT WAY TO CATCH A CHEST COLD!

Forever Cool

Appropriate Attire:

Here's a city look that's as practical as it is chic. It's sexy with full coverage!

Practical Style:

This short black jacket provides light-weight warmth.

Color That Works:

Black, with its modern, sleek uniformity, is the perfect urban color.

Great Accessories:

Her designer lightweight nylon bag is the epitome of form and function.

Never Cool

Overdoing It:

This is eccentricity taken too far. Let's hope she sees a style change in her tea leaves.

Combining Without a License:

Everything, including the kitchen sink. If you want to attain a sophisticated and cultured look, there must be a method to your madness!

Unflattering Style:

An artsy, handmade look done badly; it's everywhere! Beware!

Sad Accessories:

Are those knee-length hose?

Forever Cool 1

Something Special:

This Asian-inspired long jacket is a beautifully detailed ethnic classic.

Color That Works:

The silver in her hair and jewelry creates harmony with the navy and light blue.

The Right Shoe:

Her black leather flats are comfortable and understated. They are just the right style for a look that could have easily become costume-y.

Natural Beauty:

Keeping your hair and make-up natural and healthy looking allows you to be a bit more flamboyant with your clothes without going over the top. It's all about balance.

Forever Cool 2

Something Special:

A big and bold red triple-layer Pashmina shawl over this black suit has a dramatically stylish effect.

Great Accessories:

Her ebony jewelry is stacked front and center.

Finer Fabrics:

This is a great look when all the elements are of good quality.

Forever Cool 3

Combining With Style:

She strikes a perfect balance with the simple, modern cut of her suit and stacked silver jewelry.

Great Accessories:

Here's how more can be more. All her jewelry relates. Length, size, and material have been carefully considered. An original look that's all her own.

Color That Works:

This monotonal gray and silver theme complements her beautiful gray hair.

Never Cool

Overdoing It:

Mad Max would look low key and vulnerable next to this '80s hit!

Unflattering Style:

She's got enough hard-ware to start up a store. This hard-edged look is frightening.

UNIQUE INDIVIDUALITY WITH GREAT STYLE.

Forever Cool

Something Special:

In this outfit she struck gold!

Flattering Style:

These layered pieces create a soft, stylish look with an Eastern flavor.

The Right Shoe:

The gold ballet shoe provides the right mix of innocence and glamour.

Never Cool

Over Doing It:

Sleazeville!

Popping Out:

Reveal this much cleavage and you may never make eye contact again.

The Wrong Shoe:

Cream shoes and tan stockings will never work—with any outfit.

A Bad-Hair Day:

"Big hair" is a *Dallas* rerun.

Forever Cool

A Great Cut:

This black wool-crepe suit is tailored to create a softer look.

Great Accessories:

A Mexican silver necklace from the 1940s really lights up her face.

A Classic:

Her faux-alligator bag and black shoes complete a classic look.

Versatile Style:

This ensemble is appropriate for a luncheon or a cocktail party—even a funeral.

Never Cool

Unflattering Style:

This jumpsuit was definitely a theater curtain in its past life.

Sad Accessories:

This necklace is not quite cutting it as an "art piece"— unless you count *Return of the Blob* as art.

THE BEAUTY AND POWER OF COLOR.

Forever Cool

Creative Color:

A symphony in orange, this outfit demonstrates the power of color.

Color That Works:

These hues vary slightly, which gives the look some interest and depth as well as its unity.

Flattering Style:

In this unique look she's having a ball and having it all—glamour, sensuality, and comfortable ease.

COLOR DONE BADLY VS. ARTFUL SIMPLICITY.

Never Cool

Problem Prints:

This unbearable jacket is a walking collage posing as wearable art.

Unfortunate Color:

A perfect example of "color done badly."

Sad Accessories:

Not a drop of thought went into choosing accessories in the right style or color.

Forever Cool

Color that Works:

This black-and-white combo is simple and chic.

Figure Flatterers:

The slim cut of this blouse, with its deep v-neck, flatters her physique by elongating her neckline and upper body. A great choice for those ladies with short-waisted figures (that's 75% of us).

Combined Style:

A pair of light-weight wool-crepe slacks in black are a good investment. They will work with countless ensembles and are never out of season.

The Right Shoe and Bag:

A small designer patent-leather purse adds a bit of fun, and sexy 2-1/2" heels complete this classy look.

Never Cool

Overdoing It:

We need a permanent holiday from these "holiday" sweaters.

Sad Accessories:

These glasses give more coverage than a pair of safety goggles.

Unflattering Style:

The jeans, in pale-blue denim and the wrong cut, are most unbecoming.

The Wrong Shoe:

Standout sensible red shoes make a bad color scheme worse.

Never Cool

Repeated Offenses:

I guess her New Year's resolution wasn't to learn from her mistakes.

Forever Cool

Something Special:

Here the holiday spirit is expressed more subtly, with the festive and sophisticated colors in this unique floral-applique shawl.

Figure Flatterers:

This long black-cotton blouse fits loosely and comfortably without looking baggy.

Combined Style:

The black shirt and slacks won't compete with the bold colors of the shawl.

Great Accessories:

This vintage silver cuff bracelet and silver link necklace would go with practically anything.

The Right Shoe:

Her black-patent loafers have a simple, sleek design and a comfortable thick rubber sole.

Never Cool

Unflattering Style:

She's putting the emphasis on all the wrong places.

Underage Looks:

Even a 25-year-old would be smart to pass on this dress.

Forever Cool 1

Color That Works:

The turquoise necklace complements the cool tone of the citric-yellow sweater. The effect is clean and fresh.

Figure Flatterers:

This sweater has a long, easy fit that skims her curves perfectly. Her white slacks continue the long and graceful line.

Great Accessories:

An apple-green leather bag provides a fun, harmonious accent. The beige sandals are understated and don't compete for attention.

Forever Cool 2

Color That Works:

The brown silk-taffeta shirt is a great choice for her coloring.

Figure Flatterers:

This easy outfit just took off 10 pounds.

The Right Bag:

The colors of her outfit are repeated stylishly in the black leather and cane detail of her "Jackie O" bag.

Never Cool

A Poor Cut:

A dress that resembles a shroud.

Unflattering Style:

Even if you have phenomenal calves, asymmetrical hemlines should be avoided at any cost.

Sad Accessories:

Long, dangly earrings and eyeglasses should be mutually exclusive.

MINIMALIST CHIC—
SHEER YET FULLY COVERED.

Forever Cool

Simplicity:

Utterly simple elegance!

Great Accessories:

In keeping with a minimalist look, the Moroccan cuff bracelets are her only accents.

Figure Flatterers:

These sheer layers add interest as well as coverage (for arms and shoulders) without added weight.

The Right Shoe:

Flat shoes are perfect with this look. Heels any higher would have spoiled the lines.

Never Cool

Unflattering Style:

She's trying to look artsy, but she's coming off as decidedly uncreative.

Dated Style:

There are some towns in America where time seems to stand still and dresses like this one still grace window displays. Perhaps she should relocate?

Forever Cool

Something Special:

This short jacket, in fabric of a Seminole Indian design, suggests an artistic and confident personality.

Great Accessories:

The authentic, handcrafted silver Concho belt shares center stage.

Combined Style:

Her simple, black-wool turtleneck and fitted, boot-cut, black velvet jeans provide a sexy and subtle canvas for her bold jacket and beautiful belt.

The Right Shoe:

These black half boots with a pointed toe and a 2" heel complete a long-legged and lithe silhouette.

BLACK-TIE STYLE

"THE WAY YOU LOOK TONIGHT"

For some women nothing instills panic like those three little words: Black Tie Requested. As soon as you read the invitation, you remember that perfect dress—the one you passed up, thinking, "Where would I ever wear that?"

But, as we all know, those occasions come up eventually. Whether it's a formal dinner (even some cruises include them), an evening party, charitable event, formal wedding, or Bar Mitzvah, you'll have to come up with something. Something appropriate and, of course...absolutely amazing!

Then there are those of you (extremely social women) who are in a constant whirl of formal events: your closet is packed with floor-length dresses and glittering accessories. Perhaps it's time for a little reevaluation. As the times change, you do as well, and your evening clothes need to make the transition with you.

Ask yourself some tough questions. How is my neckline, my bust line? How are my shoulders? Can I get away with bare arms? Think about...will I be chilly? Will I be standing all night, or dancing? Considering these questions carefully may make the difference between a memorable night and one (ouch, those shoes!) you'd rather forget. Keep those thoughts in mind as you look at the photos that follow.

Just like you, the night is still young!

Never Cool

Matronly Style:

There's no denying this dowdy outfit shouts "Mother (or Grandmother) of the Bride."

Unnatural Look:

The makeup and hairstyle are overdone and seriously out of touch.

Forever Cool

Versatile Style:

Elegant and practical separates. They can be dressed up or down (proof of versatility on page 123).

Having It All:

A stylish option for ample coverage while maintaining a sexy appeal.

Color That Works:

Here's a low-key, sophisticated color scheme—but not as predictable as all black.

Natural Beauty:

Uncontrived and lovely…he can run his fingers through her hair.

Never Cool

Unfortunate Color:

Surprise, surprise! Red and black is a predictable and boring color duo that so many favor (especially at Christmas).

Unflattering Style:

This mundane jacket and dress haven't an ounce of modern style.

Body Snatcher:

The enormous glasses take full possession of her face.

Sad Accessories:

Even a thief would think twice about this purse!

Forever Cool

Great Innovation:

The convenience of contact lenses when glasses may not work (especially for these very dressy affairs).

Flattering Style:

This three-piece navy silk taffeta outfit is simple, elegant, and totally comfortable.

Color That Works:

The combined effect of this monotone palette and minimalist style creates an unbroken line that is slimming.

Natural Beauty:

Her hairstyle reveals a beautiful, high forehead that enhances her facial features.

Never Cool

Unflattering Style:

"Gypsy Woman" was a hit; this look isn't.

Unfortunate Color:

Such a wild mix of colors could induce vertigo.

Sad Accessories:

Just what this outfit deserves! A fake leather gold lamé bag and shoes.

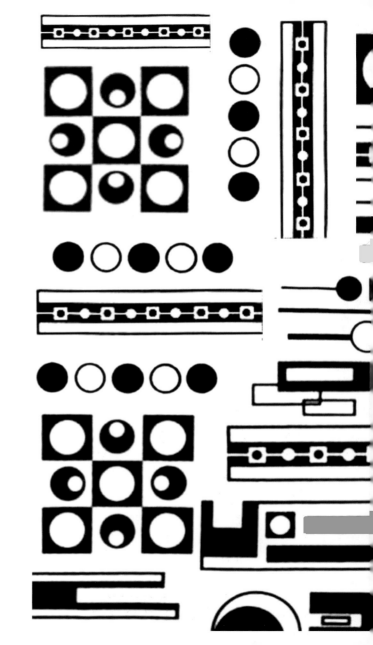

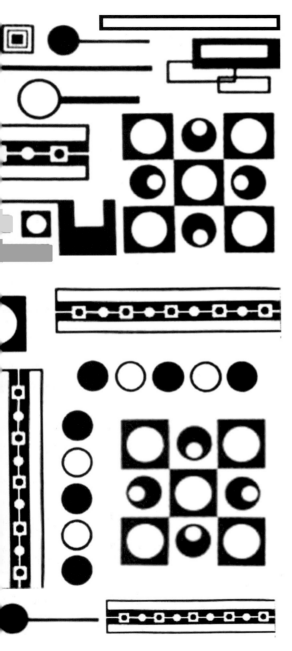

Forever Cool

Finer Fabrics:

A silver-embroidered black velvet coat provides rich texture over a simple, long silk charmeuse sheath dress.

The Right Coat:

This matching coat provides an elegant black-tie evening option for coverage and warmth.

Great Accessories:

Her comfortable, black satin flat shoes keep in stylish step with the outfit.

Never Cool

Underage Looks:

Perfect for the Junior Prom.

Sad Accessories:

Too-cute diamond jewelry. "Are you going steady?"

A Bad Hair Day:

Birds could nest in this 'do!

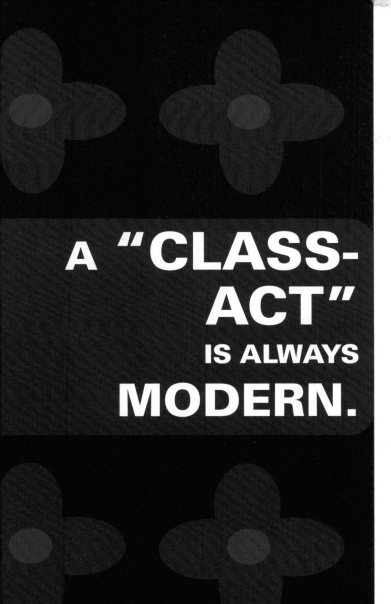

A "CLASS-ACT" IS ALWAYS MODERN.

Forever Cool

Color That Works:

An option for the "little black dress" that isn't black. Consider midnight navy for its flattering tone and chic look.

Chic Style:

Can you get more classic or modern?

Great Accessories:

The simple 14" strand pearl necklace, an elegant satin clutch, and sexy (but still comfortable) two" heeled black satin sling-back shoes are all part of a classy package.

Never Cool

Inappropriate Attire:

If Elvis were female…

Overdoing It:

This heavily sequined bolero has a blinding effect.

Poor Fabrics:

This slip dress lacks the quality satin required for a "quality" look.

Unfortunate Color:

Burgundy! An unflattering and severe color that's too popular for evening affairs.

Sad Accessories:

She never misses a "golden" opportunity! Avoid the shine, glitz and "bling."

Forever Cool

Something Special:

A look that has ease, sensuality, femininity and incredible stylishness.

Appropriate Style:

Here's a soft and sheer style that still provides coverage.

Unique Style:

A look that will separate her from the crowd, yet not so trendy that it couldn't be considered classic and virtually ageless.

ACCESSORIES

"IT'S IN THE BAG!"

There's no question—accessories define your style. All it takes is a glance at your eyeglasses, watch, bag, or (especially) shoes to know your story. Accessories—like the pillows on your couch or the paintings on your wall—can reveal a great deal about your personality. When it comes to updating your wardrobe they are the most important investment you can make—whether it's a lustrous string of pearls, a triple-layer cashmere shawl, a pair of antique earrings, a hand-stitched leather bag, or that cuff bracelet from a foreign land. Collecting accessories that you love can be great fun, and having them at your fingertips will give you pleasure time and time again. You'll always be grateful that you made the purchase.

Whether you're a minimalist at heart—or someone who likes to push the envelope—the goal is to look your most attractive while maintaining a modern youthful edge. That said, there are a few areas with potential age-related pitfalls that deserve special attention.

First consider eyewear. It has a new lease on life, and the look is definitely young! Even a hip outfit won't save you from looking old if you hold your menu at arm's length in order to see it, or peer over your "readers." If you need glasses, get them! There are hundreds of hip, modern, and affordable styles out there. Opt for a neutral colored frame that complements your face. Walk away from large red (or any "happy/artsy" color) glasses—even Sally Jesse Raphael gave hers up!

Sunglasses rate a little more leeway, but think twice about extreme or gaudy styles—you'll never go wrong with a pair in black or classic tortoiseshell.

When it comes to watches, you may need more than one (for different activities). Avoid a small ladylike watch as your primary watch—it's sure to age you. As you've seen in so many of the photos, a large, sporty, silver (almost masculine) watch is the everyday winner. Its sporty style implies activity, vitality, and youthfulness. For evening try a dressier look, perhaps in gold. Sleek and simple (without "bling" for a classier look) remains the goal.

Now, let me plead my case for the naked neckline. Unfortunately, many women think that an older neck needs concealment at all costs. One may grab any old scarf or, even worse, the sash from her dress and coil it endlessly around her neck. Who is she fooling? A well-chosen scarf can enhance an outfit, or be used for warmth, but not for hiding behind.

Reveal your neck proudly! The v-shape created by a simple cotton shirt with the top two buttons open and collar turned up will frame and elongate you neck and flatter your jawline. The result is straightforward and chic.

Keep in mind that an absence of jewelry can be surprisingly dramatic and modern. However, if you choose to wear jewelry, particularly at the neckline, consider pieces that have character and

are bold in design. Today, a wide selection of amazing jewelry is available that incorporates innovative combinations of metals, beads, stones, pearls, and gems. A spectacular necklace can enhance your neck and flatter your face. It's time to trade in those gold chains and jewelry that merely take up space.

When it comes to your bag, don't underestimate its importance—it's not just a practical necessity. The right bag will enhance the overall success of your outfit. It's wishful thinking to believe you've found a bag "for all seasons"—you need variety. Begin with a good black bag for every day, then add brown, then tan or luggage-color. By having a selection of bags (and shoes), from sporty to dressy, you can change the look of an outfit a number of times, as well as dress it up or down.

Mentioning shoes in the same breath as bags was no accident. They should complement each other and relate in style and color. Although shoes can become a challenge as we age, we don't have to sacrifice style for comfort—it just takes a bit of effort and a stylish vision of your new self.

Never Cool

Sad Accessories: She's making her "golden years" statement prematurely (there's never a right time for that!) with boring gold chains and ladylike earrings.

Forever Cool 1

Unique Accessories:

A modern silver reproduction of a '40s Mexican design brightens her face and supplies artful personality to the simplest outfit.

Forever Cool 2

Color That Works:

This multi-strand turquoise necklace brightens her complexion and enhances her blue eyes. Once again, an accessory supplies enough style and drama to make a very simple outfit superb and special.

Never Cool

The two extremes of watches—too ladylike in scale and conservative design, or the unrefined and ostentatious "bling" design.

Forever Cool

Oversized (masculine) watches have a sporty flair that is youthful, stylish, and spirited. For evening or formal affairs, smaller and more feminine watches in yellow or white gold are usually perfect.

Never Cool

Never Cool:

Round and round the scarf goes...and where it stops, nobody knows! This familiar look is an obvious attempt to hide something.

Forever Cool

Classic Style:

Her neck is strikingly framed by an upturned collar and an aqua cashmere cardigan flung about her shoulders. The classic, lustrous pearl necklace is all the adornment (not concealment) she needs.

GOOD GROOMING—"GET REAL!"

TAKING CARE OF YOURSELF

Updating your look is about looking fresh and natural. It's not about appearing completely pulled together with every strand of hair in place and makeup perfectly applied. A modern look (especially as we age) needs to be clean, simple, and relaxed. It's about toning down.

Consider the effect of shiny, freshly washed hair, cut in a flattering modern style (for a natural look, run your fingers, rather than a comb, through your hair to define your hairstyle), or pulled back in a simple ponytail. Always avoid a too "done" or "perfect" look. Combine it with makeup that has a light touch—and you've just found one secret to a youthful appearance! Sure, it may take some expertise to master the art of natural-looking makeup (unless you actually go au natural), but it can be as simple as buying the right beauty products. Explore the wide assortment of highly sheer and light foundations that "illuminate the skin" (many with SPF). Use concealer only where needed. Apply blush or bronzing power to obtain that "sun-kissed" appearance—it's a healthy, vibrant look. When it comes to your eyes, try brown or gray eye shadow and a minimum of mascara. Your brows may need some grooming but don't over do it, and use the eyebrow pencil sparingly.

Some women are lucky (yes, lucky!) to be blessed (even at an early age) with the purest shade of white hair. Although gray or white hair implies "older," being modern happily embraces a beautiful head of hair—whatever the color. If you have thick, healthy hair, it's a crime not to wear it longer (at or just below the shoulder). Who says we have to wear our hair short after 50?

If you're a blond (or choose to be), make sure your color includes multiple tones, in shades of gold. Likewise, redheads and brunettes should modulate color tones as Mother Nature might. Avoid pure black; it's harsh on an older complexion. Be sure to condition your hair often; dull and lifeless hair is aging. But, if you need help, a lightweight pomade or spray can add shine without leaving your hair greasy.

Daily moisturizing of both face and body is a must. A little experimentation with creams and lotions can help find the one best suited to your skin type.

Don't underestimate the power (at any age) of a radiant smile; it lights up your face more than any makeup. White teeth imply youthful good health. Today there are a number of dental procedures for whitening teeth, and most drugstores have a good selection of such products.

Some believe that long, deep-red fingernails are stylish and sexy, but in truth, the look is harsh and belongs with the extreme styles in some of my before photos. In fact, a short, natural-looking nail is far more refined, sensuous, and youthful—it implies an active woman who is not afraid of breaking a nail. For a bit of glamour, try a French manicure. It needs to be well done and subtle—no chalky, bright-white lines! In the case of toenails, choose either natural or neutral polish to avoid clashing with your outfit.

Last, but certainly not least—take care of yourself! With a healthy diet and proper exercise, you'll be enjoying your new look for a long time to come.

Part 3

MEN

"THE SPORTING LIFE"

When it comes to style, you men can have it so easy! For one thing, men's fashion trends don't change as often—or as drastically—as they do for women. That said, you might stumble into many of the same fashion pitfalls. You hold onto clothing for *way* too long (until it's out of fashion or no longer fits). Reevaluate your physique from time to time. Do you *really* still have a 34" waist or is it sneaking closer to 40? (Your waist is not *under* your belly.) Another misstep is borrowing extreme style ideas from the younger generation—think twice before you indulge in the excessive or outrageous.

The goal is to find comfort and style in a look that is simple, unaffected, and *masculine*. Yes, *some style*…even if you have a serious workout ethic. Whether you've been to the gym or just finished a round of golf, throw on a great warm-up jacket or pants; well-chosen layering makes all the difference as you move on to what's next on your agenda.

The following photographs highlight many options for a modern sport look. It's not about being a "fashion plate"—it's about *simplicity* in both color and style. Now that you've seen it, making your next purchase can be amazingly simple!

Never Cool

Sad Accessories:

This hat belongs on a riverboat.

Problem Prints:

We can see you coming! There's no need for such a bold, overwhelming stripe.

The Wrong Socks:

Are those socks or support hose?

Forever Cool

Great Accessories:

If you look great in hats, a baseball cap is a good choice (plenty of sun protection too).

Color That Works:

These understated colors combine exceptionally well for a look that's handsome and masculine.

The Right Socks:

These low-profile gray socks work well with the classic solid brown golf shoe.

Simplicity:

Less is once again more.

Never Cool

Inappropriate Attire:

Dressing like a "boy from the hood" won't make you an "All Star."

Overdoing It:

Tripping over your laces (the style in the local high school) will only give you scuffed knees.

Under-age Looks:

Even younger dudes have given up that hat-backward look.

LOOKING INAPPROPRIATE ONLY EMPHASIZES YOUR AGE.

Forever Cool

Finer Fabrics:

High-tech fabrics offer both form and function. They're made for sport, so why not use them?

Simplicity:

Choose pieces that are simple and low key.

Great Necklines:

The zip-up top allows ventilation and the collar frames the neck nicely.

The Right Shoe:

Choose sneakers with the latest technology. Neutral tones make them easy on the eyes.

The Right Socks:

Low-profile socks (that show barely beyond the sneaker) are the only hip option.

Never Cool

Sad Accessories:

The Lone Ranger has traded his horse for a golf cart. This hat is riding him!

Unfortunate Colors:

Ecru and pale yellow— two colors that are only right for Easter eggs.

Bad Combinations:

Paired with pastels, these black slacks create a harsh and unattractive color scheme.

The Wrong Shoe:

Those blue golf shoes are odd! Don't buy them *even on sale*.

CLASSIC SIMPLICITY CONVEYS MASCULINE CONFIDENCE.

Forever Cool

Simplicity:

Keep it clean and classic.

Color That Works:

When paired with a neutral palette, this bright green is flattering and gives a nod to Preppy fashion.

The Right Fit:

The olive khaki slacks work for his physique. If you have a small waist and athletic thighs, pleated slacks are always a good bet.

Never Cool

Underage Looks:

Juvenile emblems are for juveniles.

Unfortunate Colors:

Black may become harder to wear as we age, but can any man ever wear bright fuschia?

A Poor Fit:

That's what these shorts are.

YOU CAN SEE THOSE SHORTS COMING A MILE AWAY.

Forever Cool

Color That Works:

This heather-gray t-shirt (a staple in any wardrobe) is rugged, practical, and flattering for every complexion. It's also a good alternative to whites, which will yellow in the wash.

A Perfect Fit:

The t-shirt skims his body nicely and leaves enough room for ventilation.

The Classics:

A simple t-shirt and boxer-style shorts are basics for workouts.

Colors That Work:

This color scheme is modern and masculine.

Never Cool

Sad Accessories:

You in that hat . . . only your mother could love!

Problem Prints:

A polo shirt on acid.

Bad Style:

Short or long, these denims were never hip!

NAVY AND KHAKI CAN "MAKE THE MAN."

Forever Cool

A Classic:

This khaki baseball cap is sporty and sophisticated—now he can putt without looking like a putz.

Color That Works:

A great shade of blue can "make the man."

Combining with Style:

These olive cotton-twill shorts would go well with any color top.

Never Cool

Improper Attire:

Even if you have a great game, you'll never get any respect wearing this.

Overdoing It:

Testosterone anyone?

HORMONE OVERLOAD.

"YOU KNOW YOU'RE LOOKIN' GOOD!"

Forever Cool

Appropriate Attire:

Being grown up doesn't mean you have to compromise your appeal!

A Complete Look:

When you layer with style, you can go straight from a great win to a celebration breakfast.

Simplicity:

Sleek and simple, this high-fashion option is masculinity at its best—you know you're lookin' good!

CASUAL-STYLE

"LAID BACK"

Ask any woman and she'll agree—a man looks his sexiest and most handsome in simple, classic clothes. Think of yourself in a plain white cotton shirt and a basic pair of blue jeans. . . . See what I mean?

Unfortunately, ninety percent of Baby Boomer men (and their fathers) think that flowered or splashy print shirts are high style (sorry guys, only vintage Hawaiian shirts rate merit). This predictable, fussy—not to mention boring—look has virtually become a national uniform! Are you aware that it does nothing for your masculinity? Another notorious offender is the t-shirt and jacket combo made so popular by Don Johnson in the '80s television show, *Miami Vice*.

Men (as well as women) often cling to formula dressing that should have been retired long ago. Reassess your look at least once a year and reevaluate your choices, always striving for a classically based modern look. Study the photos in this chapter as I make my case for a simple, masculine look. You may be surprised at how simple it really is.

Never Cool

Poor Design:

Are those *3/4 length* sleeves?

The Wrong Shirt:

This look requires a classic shirt or polo, *not* a t-shirt.

Unflattering Looks:

Tucking a t-shirt into front-pleated pants does nothing to slim his waistline.

Dated Cuts:

Front pleated *denim* pants are neither jean nor trouser. They belong in no-man's-land.

Forever Cool

A Classic Look:

Ah! The relaxed and unpretentious look of the right jeans paired with a simple cotton shirt is classic and sexy.

The Right Shirt:

In white, khaki, or blue, this shirt is a winner.

The Right Shoe:

A pair of soft driving moccasins is the perfect touch for a laid-back look.

Never Cool

Outdated Style:

This '80s leather bomber jacket is a "has-been"; those oversized shoulders spell the same fate for this man.

Unfortunate Colors:

The unattractive yellow sweater can't save him either.

Dated Cuts:

The tapered jeans shorten his legs. They belong with the jacket…in another era.

A "HAS BEEN" LOOK IS NEVER RIGHT TODAY

Forever Cool

A Complete Look:

This quilted hunting jacket (lightweight and practical) paired with flat-front, straight-legged chinos (jeans or cords work, too) is a terrific look, seen often in Mediterranean countries.

Color That Works:

A medium-blue, classic-cut shirt will flatter any man's complexion!

Great Style:

Keep it simple!

LAID BACK STYLE
LAID BACK STYLE
LAID BACK STYLE
LAID BACK STYLE
LAID BACK STYLE
LAID BACK STYLE
LAID BACK STYLE

LAID **BACK** STYLE

LAID BACK STYLE
LAID BACK STYLE
LAID BACK STYLE
LAID BACK STYLE
LAID BACK STYLE

Never Cool

Outdated Look:

The t-shirt and jacket combo (the *Miami Vice* look) has become a perennial of casual dressing—a story that needs a closing chapter.

Unflattering Neckline:

Leaving the neck exposed is not a great idea as we age—give it a frame.

Poor Design:

This unstructured jacket lacks cut and style.

Forever Cool 1

Reinvention:

This *Cubano*-style shirt combines classic and ethnic into a great casual jacket for warmer weather.

A Perfect Neckline:

The combination of t-shirt and turned-up collar creates a flattering frame for the neck that reads hip and masculine.

Forever Cool 2

Youthful Alternatives:

Bridge the generation gap. These are great examples of age-appropriate pieces that your son might steal from your closet.

Finding Balance:

The shirt's simple, classic cut balances the fun, flamboyant color.

Something Different:

The black, flat-knit sweater that zips up the front is a great alternative to a jacket.

The Right Fit:

These jeans fit perfectly.

The Right Shoe:

The designer leather bowling shoe in black is trendy but simple enough not to look over-styled.

Never Cool

Scary Shirts:

Oh, man! There's that shirt again! Evidently, it's a uniform for "men of a certain age."

Overdoing It:

The hair is combed so solidly square that we suspect the Hair Club for Men.

Predictable Looks:

Way too neat and boxy; he must be guilty of something.

The Wrong Fabric:

Washed silk is comfortable but hardly masculine!

THINK OUTSIDE

"FLOWER SHIRT BRIGADE"

SIDE THE BOX

Forever Cool

Body Wise:

The simple black polo flatters and slims a burly upper torso.

Great Hair:

Combed back and slightly tousled , this hairstyle reveals a great face.

The Right Look:

Worn without a belt, the olive green cotton cargo shorts have a fashion-able but unstudied and masculine look.

The Right Shoe:

The stylish, soft, black leather loafers are the perfect choice—not too heavy for this man's sturdy frame.

ANCIENT PIECES— DUG UP FROM THE DEPTHS OF A DRAWER!

Never Cool

Unfortunate Colors:

This red is best for ketchup.

Making Do:

Buy some shorts and let these swimming trunks sink to the bottom of the pool.

The Wrong Shoe:

Could "sensible" be any more boring or unattractive?

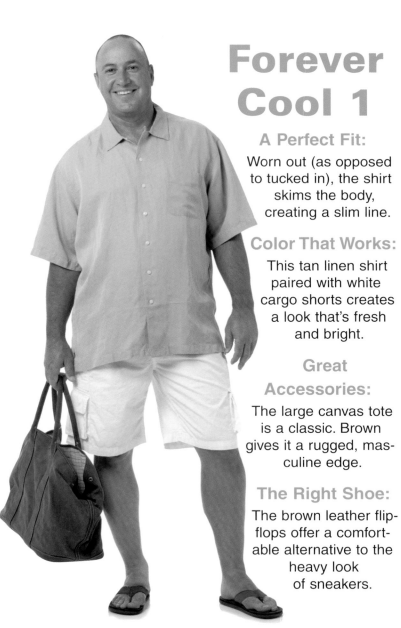

Forever Cool 1

A Perfect Fit:

Worn out (as opposed to tucked in), the shirt skims the body, creating a slim line.

Color That Works:

This tan linen shirt paired with white cargo shorts creates a look that's fresh and bright.

Great Accessories:

The large canvas tote is a classic. Brown gives it a rugged, masculine edge.

The Right Shoe:

The brown leather flip-flops offer a comfortable alternative to the heavy look of sneakers.

Forever Cool 2

Color That Works:

Again, blue does the trick. Wear it bright for a casual day look or softer with that perfect sport coat—it always complements a tan and peps up paler complexions.

Unexpected Combinations:

Complementary colors like this bright blue and orange are great together.

The Right Shoe:

Youthful flip-flops in green give this outfit a "fun color" finishing touch.

Never Cool 1

Aging Looks:

Thanks to that hat, you are now officially a Senior Citizen.

Outdated Styles:

Those ever-popular and predictable flow-ered shirts! Are the *Beach Boys* to blame?

Squeezing In:

No piece of clothing should be too tight, *especially* shorts!

Never Cool 2

Problem Prints:

Only one of the problems with this same old, same old shirt.

Double Trouble:

Socks with sandals are bad enough, but pulled up to the max? He also likes black socks and black Oxfords worn with shorts.

Forever Cool

Color That Works:

Love that blue—this time in a novel retro design that has a stylish look.

The Right Combination:

The white shorts make a simple statement, leaving center stage for the shirt.

Never Cool

Dated Look:

The colorful nylon jogging jacket is no better than it was with its matching bottoms. Keep them together— in the back of the closet.

Poor Cut:

Adding insult to injury, the raglan sleeves diminish the shoulders.

THINK LAYERS!
THINK ZIPPERS!
THINK MONO-TONES!

Forever Cool

Textured Layering:

A zippered leather jacket with nylon sleeves is worn over a simple knit sweater, under which a plain cotton t-shirt gives coverage at the neck.

Body Wise:

The sweater's short, zippered opening provides a flattering frame for the neck.

Color That Works:

This subtle but masculine color combination will work for any man. Guaranteed! The grayish-green color is amazing!

Figure Flatterers:

The slimming, flat-front brown cords are classic and add just the right texture to this stylish but unselfconscious look.

The Right Shoe:

The plain, classic suede loafers are just the ticket here.

Never Cool

Unfortunate Styles:

Popular in the '80s, this Coogie sweater belongs in the Bad Taste Hall of Fame—and the men who cling to them in the Hall of Shame.

Inappropriate Looks:

Round or v-neck sweaters worn without a visible shirt or t-shirt underneath take on a thuggish look.

Flashy Jewelry:

Gold chains, diamond earrings, and gold watches with diamonds belong to hip-hop artists or the Sopranos—not someone who'd like to be seen as refined.

A Poor Fit:

Ouch! Jeans this tight could cause some serious damage.

The Wrong Shoe:

Two-toned moccasins, webbed or otherwise, look too precious, over-styled, and are seen on way too many men's feet.

"BAD TASTE HALL OF SHAME."

THE BEST STATEMENT— HIP AND LOW-KEY.

Forever Cool

Color that Works:

Pale gray, navy, and black—masculine choices.

Something Different:

The navy suede shirt is luxe, adding interest with texture to this simple outfit. Worn over a polo it provides a stylish option to the classic jacket.

A Stylish Cut:

The jeans have a loose, modern cut.

The Right Shoe:

The black boots are practical and comfortable. As a bonus, the lug soles add height!

Good Grooming:

Hair combed back— what a difference!

Never Cool

Unfortunate Colors:

Thought probably did go into this terrible color scheme; but it came to the wrong conclusion.

Underage Looks:

Cross-generational does not mean borrowing little Tommy's sweater.

Sad Slacks:

Where do you buy pants like these? Is there an "over-the-hill" department?

The Wrong Shoe:

Only cowboy boots can tolerate leather this stiff.

Forever Cool

A Classic Jacket:

This brown suede jacket will never go out of style.

A Complete Look:

The crisp blue cotton shirt and rugged cargo pants say it all.

An Eye for Detail:

The beautiful Native American turquoise belt buckle adds a unique and personal touch.

Great Accessories:

The belt (in luggage brown) coordinates with his moccasins—as they should.

Never Cool

Dated Cuts:

Could this get any more unstructured and unattractive?

Unfortunate Colors:

Teal and burgundy?

Dated Style:

This unflattering burgundy shirt buttoned all the way up is an '80s "I'm so hip" statement.

A Poor Cut:

The teal slacks have enough fabric for a second pair.

The Wrong Shoe:

These black loafers are stiff and dainty at the same time.

PASSÉ 80'S "I'M SOOO HIP..."

Forever Cool

The Right Jacket:

This seersucker sport jacket is a classic. The inset sleeve is broad enough to maintain the shoulder line.

Color That Works:

The lime-green polo gives a summer feel to the look and enhances the complexion.

A Modern Look:

The right jeans worn without a belt are unaffected and casual.

The Right Shoe:

Yes, that moccasin works again.

PROFESSIONAL-STYLE

"BUSINESS CLASS"

When it comes to style, the world of business represents a huge playing field, and I think a little coaching is in order. Many men these days either ignore dress codes or seem to think that they don't apply. Either way, they're mistaken—there are some rules to the game.

When a man shows up in a well-fitted, navy or charcoal classic pinstripe suit, he deserves a round of applause. A man who understands fit and fabric and is armed with a refined taste will always trump the clueless one who attempts to rewrite the rules.

At times, and especially in certain professions, it's "hip to be square." Not outdated or boring, of course, but classic in foundation. In the art world they say you must learn to draw before you can create the abstract (even a talent like Picasso). The same principle works for personal style. You need to understand the basic elements of dressing well before you can "make it your own." The simplest suit, American or European in style, can be given a "twist" or be transformed into a number of outfits just by pairing it with the right (and high quality) shirts, ties, belts or suspenders, cufflinks, and, most important, shoes.

How much license you take with these combinations depends on your profession; however, you have the opportunity to look great whether you work in a formal office or one where every day seems to be "Casual Friday." Being modern is acknowledging the importance of your appearance, whether you're climbing the ladder in a competitive career or reinventing yourself in a new one. Wherever you spend your workday, the photos that follow are sure to guide and inspire you.

Never Cool

Unfortunate Colors:

This washed-out, medium-brown pinstripe suit pales his tan. So does his ecru shirt.

The Wrong Fabric:

If you could feel the stiff synthetic fabrics of his shirt and suit, you would wonder how his skin can breathe.

Sad Accessories:

He's wearing a tie that looks older than he is…and his sensible, Oxford shoes lack "form" and have only "function."

Forever Cool

The Right Suit:

This light tan suit (perfect for summer) enhances his coloring, as does this blue, spread collar, fine cotton dress shirt.

Color That Works:

Blue shirts (in checks and stripes, too) are sure to bolster any man's complexion. Other options include white (a "must" for formal business events) and light pink shirts.

Great Accessories:

His solid tan, satin-finish tie adds understated chic, while his classic, luggage-color leather oxford shoes are just right with his light suit.

Never Cool

The Wrong Suit:

This drab and boring suit will blend you into the woodwork.

Bad Combination:

This unattractive choice of a brown shirt with a loud pattern tie ignores rules of proper business attire—and will win you a job in a used car lot.

The Wrong Shoe:

These woven loafers are popular with men who wear such suits. They are a bad choice with any outfit.

Forever Cool 1

Appropriate Attire:

This single-breasted, navy pinstripe suit with peaked lapels is a winner! Its classic cut and fine workmanship ensures its longevity in his wardrobe repertoire.

The Power of Color:

The navy tie, with its simple white square pattern, paired with the blue spread collar shirt, creates a chic, monochromatic blue-on-blue look.

Great Accessories:

A white cotton pocket square is a wardrobe staple. Here it picks up the white of the suit stripe and the white pattern in the tie.

The Right Shoe:

Black leather Oxfords, maintained at a high polish, complete this classic look.

Forever Cool 2

A Classic:

A gray chalk-stripe wool flannel suit, with a classic notched lapel, is as handsome as it is practical (flannel makes great winter-weight fabric). Charcoal gray looks handsome and works as well as dark navy to flatter the complexion.

Color That Works:

The rust tie has an understated white and blue pattern, and the light blue and white cotton pocket square picks up the colors of the tie.

The Right Shoe:

He chooses a dark brown leather oxford shoe (polished to perfection) that relates to the earth tone of the tie.

YIKES! HE'S GIVING ADVICE IN THE MEN'S DEPT.?!

Never Cool

Overdoing It:

A certain rock star thought he could design ties—unfortunately, too many of his fans bought them.

Unfortunate Colors:

If you love burgundy, have a glass with dinner. Never choose it for a dress shirt.

Sad Accessories:

Aviator glasses are not hip (except as sunglasses).

Combining Without a License:

This color combo is nearly incomprehensible.

The Wrong Shoe:

Low-cut woven loafers are as popular as they are ugly.

Forever Cool 1

The Right Suit:

A blue single-breasted linen suit is a classic option for less formal professions like the film industry, advertising business or design field.

Something Special:

The pale lime green cotton shirt (a fun summer color) is unpredictably paired with a bright orange tie with a small blue print, giving a fashionable look to a simple blue linen suit.

The Right Shoe:

With this color combo, a black shoe was the only option. He chose a sleek loafer with a trendy "long toe" which reinforces the stylish look of this outfit.

Forever Cool 2

A Classic:

A single-breasted cashmere sport coat is a versatile piece, especially in a great classic color like this rich caramel. Sport coats are essential for a Casual Friday look.

Color That Works:

The pale blue shirt is worn casually without a tie, and is accented by the colors of a paisley pocket square.

Great Accessories:

Horn-rimmed glasses in the right style can have a modern look, but keep the frames small.

Combined Style:

Lightweight wool slacks in this charcoal shade will work with almost any sport coat in the cooler months.

The Right Shoe:

These dark brown Oxfords work well with this color scheme. Choose a good-quality, classic style and keep them well maintained.

DRESSED-UP STYLE

"KICK IT UP A NOTCH!"

It's not that jackets are always required, but it's important to know which occasions demand them, how to wear them, and what to wear when they aren't required. Aside from a sports jacket, it's critical to have a few other dressy pieces in your closet—not just that ten year-old dark suit that you trot out for weddings and funerals! Make sure the pieces are current and in good repair. Having a closet full of outdated or shabby clothes can give you the false impression of "wardrobe prosperity!"

A wide world of social events is out there, from dinners out, to cocktail parties, celebrations, or the theatre. If you pay attention to the nuances of fashion, you'll learn that minor changes in styling can make the difference between appearing outdated or not. Start with something classic, say, a blue blazer—then kick it up a notch with the latest cut in the best fabric you can afford.

The photos in this chapter present a wide range of refined looks. If you study the before and after photographs closely, you will begin to recognize what brings out a man's masculinity and makes him attractive. Whatever the season or occasion the question is whether you can join that endangered species—the Class Act.

Never Cool

Dated Style:

This man could have starred in *Boogie Nights.* All that's missing is the gold chain.

Unfortunate Color:

Don't enter the bull ring. This red jacket won't be missed.

Forever Cool 1

Something Special:

The Palm Beach look definitely works here, and this white jacket really sparkles!

Creative Color:

Violet (has a lot of blue in it) can be a fun option and is usually a com-plexion-flattering choice for the guys.

Color That Works:

The green pocket square adds a bit of punch and works well with purple (its comple-mentary color).

Combined Style:

These tan linen slacks provide a neutral base and maintain the light feel of the outfit.

Forever Cool 2

Creative Color:

If it's a Preppy look, pastels are just the ticket.

Color That Works:

These colors make the outfit.

The Right Shoe:

A luggage-brown loafer isn't too dark for this classic summer look.

Never Cool

Unflattering Style:

The cut of a double-breasted suit is a challenging fit, and it never looks good unbuttoned.

Inappropriate Attire:

This look only works in Vegas; keep it within the city limits.

Sad Accessories:

This is way too much "bling"! Money doesn't buy taste.

A Tired Look:

A predictable black t-shirt is as bad as a shirt unbuttoned to the waist.

Stiff Hair:

This flat, sprayed-down look belongs at Madame Tussaud's.

MONEY DOES NOT BUY TASTE.

Forever Cool

Simplicity:
An understated look gives him classic style.

A Classic:
The single-breasted cashmere sports jacket has a touch of luxe and will mix well with the rest of his wardrobe.

Color that Works:
This blue shirt in Sea Island fabric is both refined and casual.

A Great Cut:
His flat-front cotton chinos offer classic and versatile style (great for men with shorter legs).

The Right Shoe:
This loafer (with its recognizable equestrian detail) is an enduring style; with good reason.

A Good Hair Day:
With his hair combed softly back we can tell that this gentleman is attractive.

Never Cool

Making Do:

This tan nylon top is seriously lacking in style, and it's doing less than nothing to enhance its owner's look.

Unflattering Style:

Between his hairstyle and his neckline, this man has no chance.

Faking It:

These "faux-ranchero" belts (knock-off of an authentic western style) have gained unfortunate popularity.

A Poor Fit:

These washed-silk slacks are coming up short.

The Wrong Shoe:

His gladiator-style sandals should be thrown to the lions.

Forever Cool

A Good Hair Day:

We found a forehead under that hair— and another good-looking face.

Color That Works:

Blues and greens; the secret (until now) for instant handsome. Have you noticed? Men in uniform always look great— in blues, olive greens, khaki, and white.

Combined Style:

A collared shirt (which provides a frame for the neck) is paired with a casual sweater.

The Right Shoe:

These luggage-color moccasins are just what the outfit needs.

Never Cool

Squeezing In:

This teal sweater conjures up the Battle of the Bulge.

Unfortunate Color:

The bumblebee polo underneath is "bold," but definitely not "beautiful."

Dated Style:

These washed-silk slacks were popular twenty years ago; and they looked bad then, too.

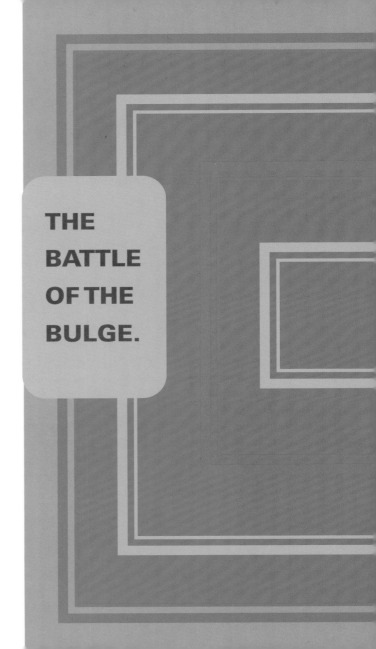

THE BATTLE OF THE BULGE.

Forever Cool

Simplicity:

This black linen shirt has a great fit and lots of potential. Paired with more black it could be quite edgy; with khakis it's simply modern.

Color That Works:

Black-and-tan is a pretty basic color scheme; here it makes for a truly hip look.

Great Accessories:

These black loafers and sleek black belt make a stylish and understated statement.

Never Cool

Problem Prints:

His boxy plaid jacket is bigger than life.

Unfortunate Color:

This pale yellow is a complete washout.

A Poor Fit:

Too much slack in the slacks!

Forever Cool

Color That Works:

Green (especially this "apple" shade) is paying major style dividends— whether it's in a pocket square, cashmere sweater, or this linen jacket.

Combined Style:

He could have worn jeans with this combo, but the white slacks really kick up the look.

The Right Shoe:

The black leather loafer works well with the midnight-navy shirt.

Never Cool

Unfortunate Color:

Pale grey is no man's friend.

Unflattering Style:

That horrid t-shirt and jacket look make a losing team.

Combining Without a License:

This light top and black slacks create a harsh contrast.

Forever Cool

Great Accessories:

He sees, and looks, better in those modern frames.

Flattering Style:

This black suit, in fine wool and current cut, is a little bit edgy and works well with his physical personality.

Creative Color:

The blue shirt with black stripe is a stylish and flattering option, and it keeps this look from being too severe.

The Right Shoe:

A black half-boot can be a hip alternative with the right outfit, but don't mix it with conservative business attire.

"READING THE CLASSICS"

It's as refreshing as it is rare these days to see a well-groomed man in a classic tuxedo. Men across the country seem to have come to the unfortunate consensus that classic formal wear is predictable and boring.

Just look at the award shows on television—they've become a circus of outlandish and garish styles. Every year our leading men (many of them old enough to know better) find some new way to put a spin on the classic tux, and each year they end up on the worst-dressed lists. The media have a field day and everyone enjoys a good laugh.

Where have refinement and class gone? It's time to restore the lost art of sophisticated formal dressing! In the photos that follow you will witness the classic tuxedo and its variables at their best—think Cary Grant.

Dare to be different—return to the classics!

Never Cool

Unflattering Style:

When men attempt to be innovative, they often end up looking like "The Usual Suspects."

Unrefined Style:

This look immediately conveys a lack of sophistication (and a possible Mafia connection).

Poor Combination:

The wrong jacket with the wrong accessories. A correct white dinner jacket is never stark white but slightly off-white—and it's a great choice for formal summer events. It must be worn with a white dress shirt with French cuffs, and a black satin bow tie.

Forever Cool

Hip to Be Square:

Invest in this classic single-breasted black tuxedo, with a peaked lapel, in lightweight worsted wool. (Owning a tuxedo is always preferable to renting one.)

The Right Stuff:

A classic white dress shirt with vertical or horizontal pleats or cotton pique front detail is worn with a black satin bow tie (the kind you tie yourself). A pure white handkerchief in your pocket is a nice finishing touch.

The Perfect Shoe:

These black leather tuxedo shoes, with a simple grosgrain detail, are a hip choice, differing slightly from the normal patent variety.

Never Cool 1

Unfortunate Style:

Another variation of the "Gangsta" look.

Wrong Fit:

His tux is an obvious rental…thanks to the wavy shoulders you could surf on.

Color Done Badly:

Looking like a card dealer at the blackjack table, he's paired a harsh, black shirt with a gold tie (don't even go there!).

Never Cool 2

Severe Style:

This hard-edged look will never qualify as a fashionable departure from classic style.

Overdoing it:

Trying so hard to be different, he winds up totally wrong!

Forever Cool

Classic With a Twist:

Here's an edgy option: a bit different, without "falling off the cliff."

Simple Style:

Choose an understated, modern version of a classic cut (tuxedo shown here with a notched lapel). Go for the best quality you can afford—it will pay dividends for years to come.

Good Combination:

For a slightly less formal look, a black satin necktie paired with a plain dress shirt and sleek leather shoes break with tradition...and it works!

BLACK-TIE
BLACK-TIE
BLACK-TIE
BLACK-TIE
BLACK-TIE
BLACK-TIE
BLACK-TIE
BLACK-TIE
BLACK-TIE
BLACK-TIE
BLACK-TIE
BLACK-TIE
BLACK-TIE

ACCESSORIES
"THE LAST DETAIL"

The number one-accessory on any man's short list would, undoubtedly, be his **watch**—it's as good a clue to his personality as handwriting analysis. The watch you choose can scream, "I'm wealthy" (think gold, encrusted with diamonds), or it can speak quietly of self-confidence with its spare elegance.

If you're looking like Mr. Magoo in oversized glasses or peering over your readers (a senior moment for sure), it's unlikely that anyone will notice your outfit, regardless of how stylish it might be. Choose **eyewear** that's modern and in a shape that flatters your face.

Always questionable—but never right on an older man—are gold chains and bracelets, ear-

rings (in one or both ears), and diamond rings. Men mistakenly believe that this kind of **jewelry** adds an aura of virility, when, in fact, it compromises your masculinity. The less-is-more standard truly applies here.

For a man who's still active in the business arena, the suit is still an important part of his wardrobe, and the **shirt** that goes with it needs great consideration. Always buy the finest quality you can afford. As a rule, blue shirts—in solids, stripes, or small checks—will flatter any complexion. A good white shirt is also a wardrobe staple. Never wear a dark shirt/light tie combination with a suit (e.g. black or burgundy shirt with a grey tie) —it's an all too common mistake. Give some thought to your collar style—whether it's a "turn-down," a "button-down," or a "spread cutaway" (the spread style will most flatter an aging neck and jawline). For your French-cuffed shirts, think about collecting unique antique cufflinks, which are usually small rather than large or garish. When considering **ties**, try pale yellow, pale silver, or navy (in either solids or small, understated prints) as your basics. Avoid ties with loud, splashy designs. If you wear **suspenders** (with or without designs), make sure they work with the color of your suit and accessories. A white handkerchief can also be a dapper addition. (see "Get Inspired!" section, p.234.) Your **belt** should always complement your shoes in style and color. A black or brown belt in plain leather with a simple buckle will work well. **Shoes** should never be considered a mere necessity or afterthought—they're a crucial part of your outfit. A classic shoe is always a safe bet (black and brown Oxfords in a "wingtip" or "cap-toe" style), but if you opt for something trendy, make sure it's well designed and understated. There are shoes for every occupation and activity. Depending on your lifestyle, you'll need to have a decent selection, not only to choose from but to avoid over-use; nothing will ruin an outfit like scuffed or down-at-the-heel shoes.

The more extensive your repertoire of accessories—those you buy each season for updating and those classics you've collected over the years—the more options you'll have for mixing-and-matching, and increasing the potential for multiple outfits whether they're casual professional or dressy.

Forever Cool

The Right Stuff:

Choose an assortment of high-end shirts, ties and pocket squares. The variety will allow you to change the look of any classic and modern fine suit

Forever Cool

Finishing Touch:

These stylish details can "separate the men from the boys"—antique silver and navy enamel cuff links, horn-rimmed glasses in a modern proportion, and a black alligator dress belt (an investment, to be sure; a fine black leather belt would be just as perfect).

Forever Cool

Pulled Together:

These suspenders have a whimsical, "Dancing Bears" print, and relate to the colors of the tie. Suspenders (or braces) serve a practical purpose and can provide an ice-breaking conversation piece. (Never wear a belt and braces together.)

Never Cool

Flashy Statement:

Your watch should never make a gaudy statement (e.g., all gold with a gold bracelet, or with any diamonds).

Forever Cool

The Right Watch:

A great watch should be considered an investment. There's a vast selection of styles, so consider your watch's compatibility with your wardrobe—its sportiness/dressi-ness factor—as well as the color of its face and band. A bracelet band, especially in a stainless steel and gold combination, along with a watch face of white or silver, is a versatile and classic style choice.

GOOD GROOMING—"WAY TO GO!"

TAKING CARE OF YOURSELF

Today, more and more men are paying attention to, and reaping the benefits of, good grooming. Taking care of oneself no longer carries implications about a man's sexual identity—it simply means keeping pace with the times. As you age, your skin, teeth, hair, and nails need greater attention, and this is a great time for changing attitudes.

Let's begin at the top. After 50, very few men still have that thick mop of hair they tried (or didn't try) to control in their 20s. What's important now is how to deal with hair loss. Yes, most drugstores carry topical lotions that may encourage hair growth, but for many men this isn't the answer. Nor are hair plugs that look like rows of corn in a field, or putting three hairs in a rubber band and passing it off as a ponytail, or the "comb-over" that's revealed for what it is every time a gust of wind comes along. And let's not forget the toupee…a "rug" whose only viable purpose can be warmth (not style). Last, but certainly not least, wearing a hat indoors doesn't fool anyone. All of these "solutions" will only advertise a man's insecurity about hair loss.

Today, younger men faced with hair loss seem to have arrived at the obvious (and most natural) solution—perhaps the only one if you want to appear confident in your masculinity—the shaved head. It's become popular (Yul Brynner was ahead of the times) and adds a dash of machismo.

If you're fortunate enough to have a full head of hair, make sure the haircut isn't overly neat (a solid mass with straight edges), or it may look suspiciously like a "piece." Combed-back hair works well on most men. For extra shine, use your fingers to run pomade lightly through your hair. The decision to "color gray away" is a personal one, but keep in mind that it most often looks obvious. If you choose the wrong color or fail to achieve a natural look, you've defeated the purpose. (A natural head of hair always has multiple shades.)

Speaking of shine, how are your "pearly whites"? Are they even white? Considering the number of options available for whiter teeth, there's really no excuse for dingy or stained teeth. It's a must for a healthy, youthful appearance.

Phew! The rest is easy.

You may have noticed that facial hair grows in and out of fashion. If you work in the business world, always think twice. Keep in mind, too, that a mustache or beard may grow in gray or white at this stage of life, and while it may add character, it may also age you.

A few final details can make all the difference: Keep your nails neat and clean. A manicure once in a while will help any man, especially if he works with his hands. If you enjoy wearing cologne or after-shave, choose something sophisticated yet understated—the ladies don't want to smell you coming. Most important, a healthy diet and plenty of exercise go a long way; good health is your ticket to good looks and good living!

Never Cool

Scary Hair:

Toupees (with rare and ultra-expensive exceptions) are obviously artificial and only inspire ridicule.

Bad Accessories:

Drugstore aviator-style glasses and gold chain necklaces are great—for 70's Halloween costumes!

Forever Cool

Natural Best:

A man is most handsome and masculine when he is unaffected, understated, and truly comfortable with his natural appearance.

Great Accessories:

These modern looking horn and wire glasses blend easily and handsomely with his features.

Part 4

SMART SHOPPING

GET INSPIRED!

"EVENTUALLY EVERYTHING CONNECTS" —Charles Eames

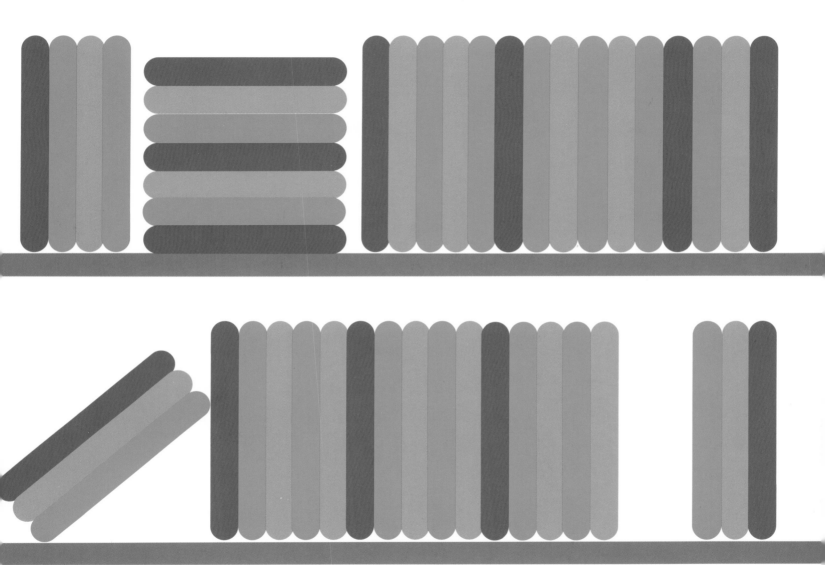

Curiosity is everything. Open your eyes! Observe all that's around you...the good and the bad...then expose yourself to "the best."

It's not about "buying power." It's about *educating your eye and refining your taste.*

Listed are some suggestions on where to look for aesthetic inspiration and knowledge (and by the way, where are your new, hip glasses? You've got some reading to do!).

MAGAZINES

TOWN & COUNTRY and TOWN & COUNTRY TRAVEL

Unsurpassed showcase for the upscale worlds of fashion, home decor, and travel...always with an unusually high standard of aesthetic value. Their pages feature what's quite pricey, but the material is worthwhile to absorb, and to use as a tool for honing your tastes.

VOGUE

This revered publication is generally good for finding the latest fashion trends. Just remember that 99% of what's currently featured may not be for you.

MEN'S VOGUE

A good new magazine that follows its big sister as a

touchstone for the latest in men's fashion. A publication for guys who need more substance than they get from *GQ* (Gentleman's Quarterly).

W

One of the most trendy upscale magazines...so again beware! It's best for inspiration, and for keeping up with what's ultra-hip.

O (The Oprah Magazine)

A great all-around women's magazine that includes some fashion and home decor. It's tasteful without necessarily going beyond the limits of imagination or budget concerns.

ARCHITECTURAL DIGEST

High-end architectural and interior design. Usually the stuff of millionaires (diverse as they may be). Something for everyone...depending on one's taste.

ELLE DECOR

Very modern and hip. This magazine also runs the gamut in design concepts—but takes time to offer ideas that are actually attainable, and not so grand.

Martha Stewart LIVING

Worth buying for the beautiful photographs alone. Even if you never undertake any of the many projects or recipes, the taste level of this magazine is so high that it qualifies as art.

BOOKS

BOBBI BROWN BEAUTY EVOLUTION by Bobbi Brown with Sally Wadyka

The best makeup and hair guide (for men too!). Bobbi's book offers a complementary philosophical companion to *Forever Cool*.

The "CHIC SIMPLE…." (A series of books) by Kim Johnson Gross and Jeff Stone

Easy to read, photo-oriented books on everything from classic fashion to bath furnishings.

THE POCKET STYLIST by Kendall Farr

Excellent style information for females of all ages.

GENTLEMAN'S GUIDE TO GROOMING AND STYLE by Bernhard Roetzel

A 101 primer on men's classic clothes, with snippets on their history.

A GENTLEMAN'S WARDROBE by Paul Keers

Another excellent guide to classic style.

DRESSING THE MAN by Alan Flusser

Such a good resource that Ralph Lauren stocks it in his men's department.

THINGS A WOMAN SHOULD KNOW ABOUT STYLE by Karen Homer

A small book dedicated to refined style for women.

HEALTHY AGING: A LIFELONG GUIDE TO YOUR PHYSICAL AND SPIRITUAL WELL BEING by Andrew Weil, M.D.

Dr. Weil, an authority on Integrative Medicine, helps to reverse the negative perception on aging while imparting excellent information on health and lifestyle. The moral of his peerless book: It isn't only about what you put on...it's also about what you take in.

YOU: THE OWNER'S MANUAL: AN INSIDER'S GUIDE TO THE BODY THAT WILL MAKE YOU HEALTHIER AND YOUNGER by Michael F. Roizen, M.D. and Mehmet Oz, M.D.

From two of the sharpest minds in medicine: a hairline-to-toenails review of what makes us tick and how a healthy lifestyle can make us the Energizer Bunnies of the best-dressed list.

PUBLISHERS

TASCHEN BOOKS

Founder Benedikt Taschen has made his small German-based imprint the worldwide home for drop-dead-gorgeous photo treatments of everything from design to fashion to exotic travel. Best news: You can afford to line your shelves with Taschen's volumes.

RIZZOLI PUBLICATIONS

Award winning, mid-priced American publisher specializing in beautiful photography of art, architecture, interiors, collectibles, gardens, and landscapes. Rizzoli's catalog is home to the beautiful people (and places, and things).

ASSOULINE PUBLISHING

With continental panache, Paris-based Assouline sees art everywhere: in our cityscapes, our divas, our video games, our race cars, our packages. Hot off the press: a 60-photograph visual history of the Barbie™ doll, and the fashion designers who contributed to her iconic look.

TELEVISION

FINE LIVING (Cable TV)

Thanks to its tasteful "lifestyle magazine" feel, this cable gem features relatively high-end pursuits...from great food and wine to decor, shopping, and travel.

MOVIES

WORKING GIRL (1988)

A wonderful send-up of the '80s which showcases the extreme styles of that era.

CASINO (1995)

This film's costumes are a monument to bad taste in all its glory.

ABOUT SCHMIDT (2002)

Remarkable for its reflections of the bland, mediocre, and even absurd style choices made by America's modern "poor-style" followers.

BARRY LYNDON (1975)

The unsurpassed costume design masterpiece of 18th-century period clothing, by the great Milena Canonero.

BREAKFAST AT TIFFANY'S (1961)

The radiant and always elegant Audrey Hepburn, looking her stylish best as Camelot dawned.

PURPLE NOON (1960)

Based upon *The Talented Mr. Ripley*, with wardrobe design so classic and hip that it looks unbelievably modern even today.

THE LAST EMPEROR (1987)

Few films can match the overwhelming splendor of this historic epic, based on the life of the last Chinese emperor. One of the movie's nine Academy Awards® went to James Acheson for Best Costume Design.

FRIDA (2001)

Julie Weiss's costumes contribute enormously to this unique, surreal film about the tempestuous life of artist Frida Kahlo.

OUT OF AFRICA (1985)

Set in 20th century colonial Kenya, the film is a tour de force by Milena Canonero, whose harmonious color and exquisite detail blur the line between painting and costume design.

SHOP GUIDE

SMART SHOPPING
GUIDE

"It's never a snap, this business of achieving a workable personal style. It takes time, patience, and energy. Why go through the whole process? Because, in the end, it's worth all the effort. Looking good is not a luxury, or an indulgence— it's an absolute necessity if you're in the game of life."

—Grace Mirabella
Editor in Chief, *Mirabella* Magazine (1989-2000)

Shopping can be fun, and also an education. We all want to avoid wasting our time and money—yet so often, we wind up doing exactly that. To better your chances of a fruitful day, here's an insider's guide to some of the best U.S. resources. Some may strike you as too pricey; but remember that exposure, curiosity, and observation are the keys to growing, staying modern, and developing great taste in clothing. So, the next time you're approached, give the answer "Just looking!" Knowing, and just seeing what's out there, is half the quest. Make it your mission to be a sophisticated consumer.

"Cool" tip: It's worth it to shoot for the best quality (not quantity) you can afford. If budget is a concern, wait for those terrific sales.

PRICE GUIDE

VERY AFFORDABLE

MID-PRICED

RATHER EXPENSIVE

VERY EXPENSIVE

FOR WOMEN ONLY

BERGDORF GOODMAN
www.bergdorfgoodman.com
Fifth Avenue at 58th Street
New York, New York 10019
212-753-7300

DOSA
mail@dosainc.com
107 Thompson Street
New York, New York 10012
212-431-1733

EILEEN FISHER
www.eileenfisher.com
29 Eileen Fisher stores in the U.S.
Also at specialty stores and most department stores

ELIZABETH LOCKE JEWELRY
(at Peipers + Kojen)

968 Madison Avenue at 76th Street
New York, New York 10021
212-744-7878

KATE SPADE
www.katespade.com
Kate Spade stores located throughout the U.S. as
well as internationally
Also at specialty shops and department stores

LINDA DRESNER
infony@lindadresner.com
484 Park Avenue
New York, New York 10022
212-308-3177

infomi@lindadresner.com
299 West Maple Road
Birmingham, Michigan 48009
248-642-4999

MANOLO BLAHNIK SHOES
31 West 54th Street
New York, New York 10019
212-582-3007
Also at Bergdorf Goodman and Neiman Marcus

MARNI
www.marni.com
161 Mercer Street
New York, New York
212-343-3912

8460 Melrose Place
Los Angeles, California
323-782-1101
Also at Neiman Marcus, Bergdorf Goodman,
and selected Saks Fifth Avenue stores

MAX MARA
SPORTMAX is the sporty, lower-priced division
MARINA RINALDI features larger-sized styles
Max Mara stores located throughout the
U.S. as well as internationally
Also at Saks Fifth Avenue, Bergdorf Goodman,
and selected Neiman Marcus stores

MIKIMOTO PEARLS
www.mikimoto.com
Four stores in the U.S.: New York, Las Vegas, and
Beverly Hills, and Costa Mesa, California
Also at specialty stores, and Saks Fifth Avenue
Other stores located in Japan, France, Hong Kong,
and the U.K.

PIAZZA SEMPIONE
piazzasempione.com
At Saks Fifth Avenue, Bergdorf Goodman,
and Neiman Marcus

REBECCA COLLINS JEWELRY
At Neiman Marcus

ROBERT CLERGERIE SHOES
www.robertclergerie.com
681 Madison Avenue
New York, New York 10021
212-207-8600

108 North Robertson Boulevard
Los Angeles, California 90048
310-276-8907
Also at Barneys New York, Neiman Marcus,
and Bergdorf Goodman

SIGERSON MORRISON SHOES
www.sigersonmorrison.com
Stores in Los Angeles, California,
and in New York City and Sag Harbor, New York

SPRATLING JEWELRY
www.sherriemathieson.com
www.spratlingsilver.com

TALBOT'S
www.talbots.com
Talbot stores throughout the U.S. as well as in
Canada, U.K., and Japan

ZORAN
www.saksfifthavenue.com
At Saks Fifth Avenue stores throughout the U.S.
800-871-SAKS (7257)

FOR MEN AND WOMEN

AGNÉS B

www.agnesb.fr
7 Agnés B stores in the U.S.: New York (4), as well as Boston, Los Angeles and San Francisco

ARMANI

www.giorgioarmani.com
Armani stores located throughout the U.S.
Also at Saks Fifth Avenue, Bergdorf Goodman, and Barneys New York

BARNEYS NEW YORK

www.barneys.com
6 stores in the U.S.: New York City and Manhasset, Long Island, New York; Chestnut Hill, Massachusetts; Beverly Hills; Chicago; and Seattle
212-753-7300 (NYC flagship store)

BROOKS BROTHERS

www.brooksbrothers.com
Brooks Brothers stores located throughout the U.S.

BURBERRY

www.burberry.com
Burberry stores located throughout the U.S. as well as internationally
Also at Neiman Marcus and Saks Fifth Avenue

CALVIN KLEIN

www.calvinklein.com
Calvin Klein Store
654 Madison Avenue
New York, New York 10021
212-292-9000

CARTIER WATCHES AND JEWELRY

www.cartier.com
653 Fifth Avenue
New York, New York 10021
800-CARTIER (227-8437)

ETRO

4 Etro stores in the U.S.
Also at Bergdorf Goodman, Neiman Marcus, and Saks Fifth Avenue

FRED SEGAL

8118 Melrose Avenue
West Hollywood, California 90046
323- 651-4129

GUCCI

www.gucci.com
Gucci stores located throughout the U.S. as well as internationally

HERMES

www.hermes.com
14 Hermes stores in the U.S.
Scarves at Neiman Marcus and Bergdorf Goodman
800-441-4488

IWC WATCHES

www.iwc.ch

JIL SANDER

www.jilsander.com
11 E. 57th Street
New York, New York 10019
212-838-6100
Also at Bergdorf Goodman, and Barneys New York

KORS BY MICHAEL KORS

www.michaelkors.com
3 Michael Kors stores in the U.S.: New York City and Manhasset, Long Island, New York; and Beverly Hills. Other locations internationally
Also at Bergdorf Goodman, Saks Fifth Avenue, Neiman Marcus and Nordstrom's

LACOSTE

www.lacoste.com
At Lacoste stores throughout the U.S. as well as internationally
Also at Bergdorf Goodman, Neiman Marcus, Saks Fifth Avenue, and Nordstrom's

LOUIS BOSTON

www.louisboston.com
234 Berkeley Street
Boston, Massachusetts 02116
617-262-6100

LUCKY BRAND

www.luckybrandjeans.com
Lucky Brand Stores
800-964-5777

LORO PIANA

www.loropiana.com
10 Loro Piana stores in the U.S.; other locations internationally
212-980-7961
Also at Neiman Marcus, and Bergdorf Goodman

MITCHELL'S / RICHARDS

670 Post Road East
Westport, Connecticut 06880
203-227-5165

359 Greenwich Avenue
Greenwich, Connecticut 06830
203-622-0551

NEIMAN MARCUS
www.neimanmarcus.com
30 stores in the U.S.
888-888-4757

NIKE
www.nike.com
Nike stores throughout the U.S. as well
as internationally
Also at specialty shops and department stores

NORDSTROM'S
www.nordstrom.com
143 stores in the U.S.
888-282-6060

PRADA
www.prada.com
11 Prada stores located throughtout the U.S.
as well as internationally
Also at Neiman Marcus, and Saks Fifth Avenue

PUCCI
www.pucci.com
3 stores in the U.S.: New York City, Las Vegas,

and Palm Beach; other stores internationally
Also at Bergdorf Goodman, Neiman Marcus,
and Saks Fifth Avenue

PUMA ATHLETIC WEAR
www.puma.com
At specialty stores and department stores

RALPH LAUREN
www.polo.com
Ralph Lauren stores located throughout the U.S.
as well as internationally
Also at most department stores
LAUREN ( **)** is the large-size label.

RLX
www.polo.com
501 East Cooper Avenue
Aspen, Colorado
970-925-5147
Also at Ralph Lauren stores in the U.S.

ROLEX WATCHES
www.rolex.com

SAKS FIFTH AVENUE
www.saks.com
611 Fifth Avenue (flagship store)

New York, New York 10022
60 stores in the U.S.
877-551-SAKS

SALVATORE FERRAGAMO
www.salvatoreferragamo.com
Salvatore Ferragamo stores throughout the U.S.
as well as internationally
Also at Neiman Marcus, and Saks Fifth Avenue

THEORY
www.theory.com
www.shopbop.com
8 Theory stores in the U.S.; other locations
internationally
Also at Neiman Marcus, Bergdorf Goodman,
Saks Fifth Avenue, Barneys New York, Macy's
West, Marshall Field, Belk's, and Nordstrom

TOD'S
www.tods.com
9 stores in the U.S.
800-4-JPTODS
Also in Bergdorf Goodman, Neiman Marcus,
and Saks Fifth Avenue

TSE CASHMERE
827 Madison Avenue

New York, New York 10021
800-487-3692

60 Maiden Lane
San Francisco, California 94108
800-873-2330
TSE stores also located in Palo Alto
and Costa Mesa, California
Also at Neiman Marcus, Bergdorf Goodman,
and Saks Fifth Avenue

WILKES BASHFORD
www.wilkesbashford.com
4 stores in California: San Francisco; Palo Alto; Mill
Valley; and St. Helena
415-986-4380 (San Francisco flagship store)

STORES FOR "TRICKLE-DOWN" STYLE

ANN TAYLOR
www.anntaylor.com
Ann Taylor stores located throughout the U.S.
800-DIAL-ANN

BANANA REPUBLIC
www.bananarepublic.com
Banana Republic stores located throughout the U.S.
800-BR-STYLE (277-8953)

COACH

www.coach.com

Coach stores located throughout the U.S. as well as internationally

Also at major department stores

COLE HAAN

www.colehaan.com

Cole Haan stores located throughout the U.S.

Also at major department stores

JCREW

www.jcrew.com

JCrew stores located throughout the U.S.

NINE WEST SHOES

www.ninewest.com

Nine West stores located throughout the U.S. as well as internationally

TARGET (ISAAC MIZRAHI FOR TARGET)

www.target.com

Target stores located throughout the U.S.

CATALOGS

ATHLETA

www.athleta.com

888-322-5515

AS WE CHANGE

www.aswechange.com

800-203-5585

BLISS

www.blissworld.com

888-243-8825

J. CREW

www.jcrew.com

800-562-0258

BRA SMYTH

www.brasmyth.com

800-BRA-9466

FOOTSMART

www.footsmart.com

800-870-7149

GORSUCH SKIWEAR

www.gorsuchltd.com

800-525-9808

NIKEWOMEN

www.nikewomen.com

888-599-6453

MORE ON-LINE RESOURCES

www.bluefly.com

www.net-a-porter.com

www.eluxury.com

FOR MEN ONLY

ALDEN SHOES
www.aldenshoe.com
www.aldenshop.com
Alden stores located throughout the U.S. as well as internationally
Also at specialty stores and Nordstrom

ALLEN-EDMONDS SHOES
www.allenedmonds.com
Allen-Edmonds stores located throughout the U.S. as well as internationally
Also at specialty stores, Nordstrom, and Dillard's

BERGDORF GOODMAN  MEN'S STORE
www.bergdorfgoodman.com
745 Fifth Avenue
New York, New York 10019
212-753-7300

CHURCH'S ENGLISH SHOES
www.churchsshoes.com
3 Church's English Shoes stores in the U.S.;

other locations internationally
1-888-99-SHOES (997-4637)

*CROCKET AND JONES  SHOES
www.crockettandjones.co.uk
c/o Turnbull And Asser Store
42 East 57th Street
New York, New York 10022
212-752-5700
Stores also in London (4) and Paris (2)

HICKEY-FREEMAN
www.hickeyfreeman.com
2 Hickey-Freeman stores in New York City
888-603-8968
Also at specialty shops and department stores throughout the U.S.

HUGO BOSS
www.hugoboss.com
Hugo Boss stores located throughout the U.S. as well as internationally
Also at specialty shops and department stores

IKE BEHAR SHIRTS

www.ikebehar.com
At specialty stores and Nordstrom, Neiman
Marcus, Saks Fifth Avenue and Bergdorf Goodman
Also available in stores in Canada and Japan

*LUCIANO BARBERA

www.lucianobarbera.it
212-315 9500
At Bergdorf Goodman

*PAUL SMITH

www.paulsmith.co.uk
Paul Smith
108 Fifth Avenue New York 10011 NY
212-627-9770
Also at Neiman Marcus, Barneys New York,
Bergdorf Goodman, and Saks Fifth Avenue

*PAUL STUART

www.paulstuart.com
2 Paul Stuart stores In The U.S.:
New York 800-678-8278
Chicago 800-227-4990
Also in Tokyo

JW WESTON SHOES

812 Madison Avenue
New York, New York 10020
212-535-2100

*ROBERT TALBOTT SHIRTS

www.roberttalbott.com
3 stores in the U.S.; other
locations internationally
212-751-1200
Also at specialty stores and
Nordstrom

JOHN LOBB SHOES

www.johnlobbltd.co.uk
680 Madison Avenue
New York, New York 10019
212-888-9797

*THOMAS PINK

www.thomaspink.com
Thomas Pink stores throughout the U.S.
as well as internationally
888-336-1192

TRAFALGAR SUSPENDERS AND BELTS

At specialty stores and Nordstrom

*TURNBULL & ASSER SHIRTS

www.turnbullandasser.com
42 East 57th Street
New York, New York 10022
877-887-6285
9633 Brighton Way
Beverly Hills, California 90210
310-550-7600
Also at Bergdorf Goodman and Neiman Marcus
Flagship store in London

ZEGNA

www.zegna.com
Zegna stores located throughout the U.S.
as well as internationally

Also at Bergdorf Goodman, Neiman Marcus, Saks Fifth Avenue, and Barneys New York

* Recommended mostly for men, but also feature some women's merchandise.